D1196083

MODERN WORLD NATIONS

Sudan

DISCARD

Joseph R. Oppong

Series Editor
Charles F. Gritzner
South Dakota State University

CHELSEA HOUSE
P U B L I S H E R S
An imprint of Infobase Publishing

Frontispiece: Flag of Sudan

Cover: The Meroë pyramids of the Kushite rulers

Sudan

Copyright © 2010 by Infobase Publishing
All rights reserved. No part of this book may be reproduced or utilized in any form
or by any means, electronic or mechanical, including photocopying, recording, or by
any information storage or retrieval systems, without permission in writing from the
publisher. For information, contact:

Chelsea House
An imprint of Infobase Publishing
132 West 31st Street
New York NY 10001

Library of Congress Cataloging-in-Publication Data
Oppong, Joseph R.
  Sudan / Joseph R. Oppong.
      p. cm. — (Modern world nations)
  Includes bibliographical references and index.
  ISBN 978-1-60413-620-3 (hardcover)
  1. Sudan—Juvenile literature. I. Title. II. Series.

  DT154.6.O66 2010
  962.4—dc22

                                    2009048066

Chelsea House books are available at special discounts when purchased in bulk
quantities for businesses, associations, institutions, or sales promotions. Please call
our Special Sales Department in New York at (212) 967-8800 or (800) 322-8755.

You can find Chelsea House on the World Wide Web at
http://www.chelseahouse.com

Text design by Takeshi Takahashi
Cover design by Alicia Post
Composition by EJB Publishing Services
Cover printed by Bang Printing, Brainerd MN
Book printed and bound by Bang Printing, Brainerd MN
Date printed: April 2010
Printed in the United States of America

10 9 8 7 6 5 4 3 2 1

This book is printed on acid-free paper.

All links and Web addresses were checked and verified to be correct at the time of
publication. Because of the dynamic nature of the Web, some addresses and links
may have changed since publication and may no longer be valid.

Table of Contents

Sudan

Introducing Sudan

Sudan is a country unlike any other in Africa. It is huge in area. Physically and culturally it is a very diverse land, and few places in the world have experienced a longer and more bitter history of conflict. Most of its people, particularly those living in the south, live in grinding poverty. Because of the widespread hardships, the Sudanese suffer from some of the worst health conditions in the world. As an added hazard, they live in fear of stepping on land mines, a potential reminder of the country's long history of deadly conflicts. The International Criminal Court (ICC) has formally charged Sudanese president Omar al-Bashir with war crimes. Al-Bashir faces arrest if he ventures outside the country. Yet Sudan's fortunes may have taken a turn for the better. The country has emerged as a potentially rich oil producer. China has already invested huge amounts of money in the development of this vital resource. This book is about the complex story of Sudan, a country that constantly struggles to survive.

From the varieties of soil on the Sudanese landscapes to the cultural practices of the Sudanese people, Sudan is a land of incredible diversity. Muslim in the north and a mix of native and Christian faiths in the south, Sudan is full of religious and many other cultural differences. As often as not, these differences have been the source of conflicts. In fact, for much of its existence as an independent country, Sudan has been trapped in civil strife. These conflicts have killed millions of people and forced even larger numbers out of their homeland as refugees. And in Darfur and elsewhere in the southern region of the country, the massacres continue today.

Sudan is as huge as it is diverse. It has an area of 967,500 square miles (2,505,813 square kilometers), nearly one-quarter the area of the United States. This makes it the largest country in Africa. Within this large territorial expanse is an amazing diversity of natural environments. It is home to enormous deserts, majestic mountain ranges, soggy swamps and marshes, and colorful tropical rain forests. From the fertility of the Nile Valley to the barrenness of the deserts, and from the poverty of the south to a north that is wealthy by comparison, Sudan is a country that offers incredibly sharp contrasts.

To prosper, a country needs an easy outlet to the rest of the world. Sudan is not landlocked. The northeastern part of the country faces the Red Sea, where Port Sudan is a major seaport facility. Yet most of the country's people and economic activity are located more than 1,000 miles (1,600 km) from the sea. The southern provinces are so far removed from the country's railroad network and Port Sudan that they use another route. They find it easier, faster, and cheaper to ship their products by rail through neighboring Uganda and on to Kenya's major seaport at Mombassa.

The country's geographic location in northeastern Africa extends from the southern border of Egypt to the northern border of Uganda, a distance of about 1,200 miles (2,000 km). In all, it shares political boundaries with nine other countries.

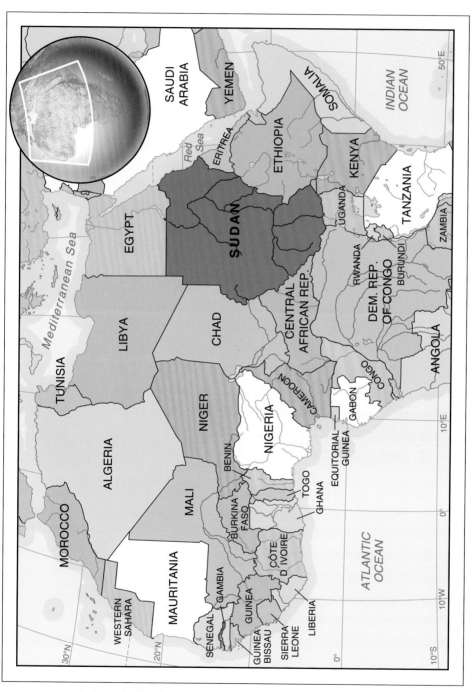

Sudan, which is located in northeastern Africa, is the largest country on the continent. Covering an area of 967,500 square miles (2,505,813 sq km), slightly more than one-quarter the size of the United States, Sudan is the tenth largest country in the world by area.

In addition to Egypt and Uganda, portions of its territory border Libya, Chad, the Central African Republic, the Democratic Republic of the Congo, Kenya, Ethiopia, and Eritrea. Many of these neighbors are also troubled by conflict. This area of Africa is an often-dangerous neighborhood. It lies astride the transition between the North African and Middle Eastern culture realm to the north and the sub-Saharan African culture realm to the south. In fact, Sudan is considered a cultural bridge that links Arabs and Africans in one huge and diverse country. This diversity is one factor that plays a key role in causing the country's seemingly ceaseless conflicts. The country combines the peoples and cultures from two quite different worlds with different ways of life. Differences include religion, language, social interactions, diet, and much more.

Sudan provides a terrific opportunity to explore many complex and currently hot topics in physical and human geography. Using Darfur, we will examine the role of possible climate change, particularly as it affects rainfall, as a factor that may influence political crisis and ethnic hostilities. We will answer the question of whether climate change, alone, can cause war. We will also explore the issues surrounding Africa's refugee crisis. You will meet children your age, who were captured as slaves, and forced to marry at ages as young as 12 years. You will encounter child soldiers. Of greatest importance, you will meet people who are trying to begin their lives again after the devastation of war.

Sudan is a country deeply divided in many ways. Because of its distribution of power and population, Sudan is a story of growth in the north and widespread despair in the south. The Muslim north is the dominant region in terms of population, political control, and economic power. Its people enjoy a fairly decent level of well-being. The weak, impoverished, and tense south, on the other hand, has always resisted northern rule and dominance. In fact, Sudan was caught in a two-decade civil war between the mainly Muslim north and the south, where people are mostly animist (the belief that spirits inhabit natural objects) or Christian. This north-south civil war lasted

21 years, and killed an estimated 1.5 million people. It finally ended in 2005.

Bitter fighting broke out in the western region of Darfur in early 2003. In Darfur, the United Nations (UN) believes that more than 2 million people have fled their homes and more than 200,000 have been killed. Today, southern Sudan looks for leadership and assistance from neighboring Uganda and Kenya, rather than to Sudan's capital, Khartoum, or the Middle East.

Since ancient times, Sudan has been an arena for interaction between the cultural traditions of Africa and those of the Mediterranean world. In recent centuries, Islam and the Arabic language have become dominant in many northern parts of the country. Arabic is the official language and Islam is the country's major religion, but Sudan also has a large non–Arabic speaking and non-Muslim population. Older and more traditional African cultural practices, including language and religion, dominate in the south. Christians and animists living in the south have rejected attempts by the government in Khartoum to impose Islamic law called Sharia on the country as a whole. In addition, Sudan (particularly in the south) has hundreds of ethnic and tribal subdivisions and language groups. This makes real partnership within the country a significant political challenge.

The two main divisions—north and south—are sharply divided along linguistic, religious, racial, and economic lines, and these divisions have generated ethnic tensions and clashes on numerous occasions. Moreover, the geographical isolation of Sudan's southern African peoples has prevented them from participating fully in the country's political, economic, and social life.

Sudan has had numerous changes in government since the country gained independence in 1956. Consecutive government rulers found it difficult to win general acceptance and support from the country's diverse population. In fact, following independence, it took the country 17 years—until 1973—to draft a formal constitution!

Seemingly constant conflict has tattered Sudan's ability to provide basic services to its people. This has caused many refugees to flee. But Sudan has also received large numbers of refugees from neighboring countries, primarily Ethiopia and Chad, both of which have their own civil conflicts. Clearly, huge numbers of people in Sudan desperately need humanitarian assistance, but armed conflict, poor transportation routes and facilities, and lack of government support continually block such attempts to help affected populations. Despite large areas of land that are suitable for cultivation, poverty and hunger are widespread among Sudan's refugees and displaced people. In addition, some southerners who once fled their homes have since returned, meaning that there is a pressing need for reconstruction. This makes the story of Sudan one of heartbreak and of a desperate struggle for survival.

Sudan has been labeled as both a terrorist state and a failed state (a place characterized by social, political, and economic failure). Two reasons probably account for this. First, did you know that al Qaeda was founded in Sudan? In fact, Sudan was the first headquarters of al Qaeda, the international terrorist organization led by Osama bin Laden. After creating the organization in 1989, bin Laden and al Qaeda operated from a Sudanese base until 1996. During this period, al Qaeda established networks with other terrorist organizations. With their help and that of its Sudanese hosts, al Qaeda grew to become a global terrorist organization.

The country was an ideal location for the terrorist organization for several reasons. First, al Qaeda prefers lawless areas with limited government (or a government that it can control). In such an environment, it can operate freely and in secret. Second, because of Sudan's size and vast area of sparsely populated desert, it is a perfect setting for terrorist training camps. Finally, the Sudanese government was weak, but supportive of what bin

Laden was doing. In May 1996, following U.S. pressure on the Sudanese government, bin Laden moved al Qaeda's headquarters to Afghanistan, where he forged a close relationship with the Taliban rulers. But for all practical purposes, al Qaeda was born and raised in Sudan. This is why the country gained its reputation as a terrorist state.

Sudan has also earned its reputation as a failed state. The International Criminal Court (ICC) has formally charged Omar al-Bashir, Sudan's president since 1993 (and still in office as of 2010) with war crimes and crimes against humanity. An international warrant has been issued for his arrest. The ICC holds President al-Bashir and his government responsible for causing the conditions that made possible the murder, rape, torture, and displacement of large numbers of civilians in Darfur. In theory, al-Bashir can be arrested if he ventures outside Sudan. In reality, that is not very likely to happen if he limits his travels to countries that support his policies. The numerous conflicts in Sudan, and the perceived involvement of the country's leaders in supporting and exploiting these conflicts, make Sudan a failed state.

In certain ways, Sudan seems to be in the Dark Ages. If a woman were to wear blue jeans in public, she could be arrested and flogged with 40 lashes. One teacher learned to her dismay that there was a price to pay of six months in jail and 40 lashes for allowing her class to name a teddy bear "Muhammad." (These two examples are discussed at length in Chapter 7.)

Sudan suffers the tragic legacy of its conflicts in numerous ways. For example, the country is dotted with dangerous and potentially deadly landmines. During the country's many conflicts, thousands of landmines were planted. During the rainy season, the mines and other hidden, unexploded devices are exposed at the surface, where they pose a great threat to civilians, especially children. One such catastrophic case took place in July 2009, when a landmine seriously injured a seven-year-old boy named Hassan. On his way back from school,

Due to the civil wars in Sudan, millions of people have been killed, injured, or displaced. People face risks daily not only from soldiers but from landmines that have been planted in tufts of grass or in soil, under fruit trees, and near water sources. Above, a Sudanese landmine victim watches others play wheelchair basketball at the Kakuma refugee camp in Kenya. Kakuma houses refugees who have fled internal conflicts in Sudan.

Hassan saw a shiny metal object sticking up out of the soil. As he attempted to pull the object from the soil, it exploded. His family immediately brought him to the nearby Doctors Without Borders hospital, where a team provides surgical care and other health services.

Hassan's two hands were completely destroyed and had to be amputated at the elbows. He had injuries to his face, eyes, neck, chest, and abdomen, and also on one of his legs. Hassan also lost his eyesight. Although his parents were happy that he survived, they were also worried about his future. He was still a strong boy, but they wondered what future he would have in a country where surviving under normal circumstances is already very difficult.

Unfortunately, in March 2009, Doctors Without Borders was one of the non-governmental organizations (NGOs) that were thrown out of Sudan when the International Criminal Court announced its charges against President al-Bashir. The Sudanese government stated that it was unable to ensure the safety of foreigners and Sudanese nationals who were not from Darfur. Doctors Without Borders teams had been working in Sudan since 1978, providing emergency medical humanitarian assistance. In addition to frequent outbreaks of violence and attacks in the region, malnutrition is widespread and the nation's maternal mortality rates remain among the highest in the world. Tuberculosis and other diseases, such as meningitis, measles, cholera, and malaria, also are rampant within the country.

Despite its historical ties to terrorism, internal conflicts, and Islamic extremism, there is some room for optimism. Sudan has gained recent importance as a potentially rich oil producer. The country's deposits are believed to hold Africa's greatest unexploited oil resources. By some estimates, Sudan's oil reserves are even greater than those of the Gulf of Guinea including Nigeria, Gabon, Ghana, and the Ivory Coast combined. In fact, some experts even suggest that Sudan's untapped oil reserves equal those of Saudi Arabia. Furthermore, Sudan has large deposits of natural gas, one of the three largest deposits of high-purity uranium in the world, and the fourth largest deposits of copper.

This newly discovered wealth has made Sudan a major center of attention of the global superpowers. The United States, however, is largely out of the running among those countries that will benefit from Sudan's resources. Because of the atrocities in Darfur, the United States imposed economic sanctions on Sudan in 2007. Instead, China is providing the technology for exploration, drilling, pumping, and the building of a pipeline. China also buys much of Sudan's oil, with payment including weapons as part of the exchange.

While U.S. oil companies are barred from operating in Sudan, China has found a reliable ally and an important oil provider in Sudan. This situation, of course, has critical implications for the global economy and political landscape. To satisfy its growing appetite for oil, the rapidly growing Asian economic giant ignores Sudan's atrocities and President al-Bashir's dismal record of leadership. In 2009, an estimated 6 percent of China's oil imports were from Sudan, and China wants more. China has already made huge investments in Sudan and other projects are planned. Currently, Asian oil companies dominate the field in Sudan. As global oil shortages increase, Sudan is going to become an even more important country.

All these conditions and more are to follow in the pages of this book. Sudan invites you into its fascinating and frequently turbulent world. Will you listen to its story?

[Note: The country of Sudan is not to be confused with the rather vaguely defined geographical region of Sudan (Arabic: *Bilad-es-Sudan,* "country of the blacks"). The latter region generally is recognized as coinciding with arid and semiarid areas of North Africa that are dominated by dark-skinned people of the Islamic faith.]

2

Physical Landscapes

S udan spans 18 degrees of latitude, a distance of about 1,250 miles (2,000 km). Located at about 4° North Latitude, its southern extremity lies very near the equator. The northern border is located at about 23° North Latitude, near the Tropic of Cancer. Everywhere one travels in Sudan, he or she will be surprised by the country's varied natural landscapes. Within the country's 967,500-square-mile (2,505,813-square-kilometer) area are found an incredible variety of physical conditions.

Land features range from boringly flat plains to rugged mountains. In the north, vast expanses of parched desert landscapes stand in sharp contrast to the rain-drenched south. The country boasts a wide array of flora (plants) and fauna (animal life). Flora reflects precipitation, which diminishes from south to north. There are lush tropical rain forests in the southern highlands. Moving northward, woodlands gradually give way to savanna landscapes, then scrub and short grasslands, and finally to scant and scattered desert vegetation in the north. In the northeast, Sudan faces upon the Red Sea. The interior's well-watered river basins of the Nile and its tributaries stand in marked contrast to the bone-dry desert conditions of the eastern Sahara.

Sudan's physical environment presents both opportunities and challenges to the country's people. Animals are biologically adapted to their habitats, the natural conditions in which they can survive. Humans, on the other hand, draw upon culture as our survival mechanism. We are able to culturally adapt to, use, and modify the physical places in which we live. Rather than nature determining how people live, people determine how useful the environment will be to them. In this chapter, you will learn about Sudan's varied environmental conditions. Elsewhere, you will find out how people have adapted to and used the land from place to place.

LAND FEATURES

To picture Sudan's land features, it is helpful to think of a horseshoe with the open end facing northward toward Egypt. The space within the horseshoe is relatively low in elevation and quite flat in terrain. In the interior, the Nile River and its tributaries flow from south to north. The streams flow through a valley that varies in width from very broad in the south to just miles in width in some northern areas. Moving from the center toward the country's edges, elevations rise. Except in the open north, the horseshoe itself is formed by the various mountain ranges that flank much of Sudan's borderland.

Highlands

Highest elevations occur in the south, near the Ugandan border. There, in the Imatonge Range, Mount Kinyeti rises to an elevation of 10,456 feet (3,187 meters). The Imatonge and nearby Dongotona mountains are the rainiest areas of Sudan and are shrouded in dense tropical rain forests. Because of the moisture, many streams flow from the highlands (including those of neighboring Ethiopia) and help form southern Sudan's huge area of marsh and swamp. In western Sudan's Darfur region, Jebel Marra rises to an elevation of 10,131 feet (3,088 m). Within Sudan, most of the southeast is lowland plain. But towering peaks within Ethiopia and Eritrea rise very near the border. In the northeast, much of the Red Sea coast is bordered a short distance inland by mountains that run parallel to the sea. In the far northeast and within sight of the Red Sea, Jebel Erba rises like a towering giant from near sea level to an elevation of 7,274 feet (2,217 m).

A hill named Jebel Barkal is located along the Nile River about 250 miles (400 km) north of Khartoum. Standing only about 300 feet (100 m) tall, it is not a major physical feature. But the landform is of great historical significance. About 1000 B.C., the area became the center of the powerful Kingdom of Kush. Archaeologists have found the ruins of 13 temples and 3 palaces, including the famous Temple of Amun that is considered sacred even today by many people. Because of its historical importance, the many ruins at the foot of Jebel Barkal are now a UNESCO World Heritage Site.

Lowlands

Most of the country's interior is quite flat, with plains and low plateaus occupying much of the area. In the northern roughly half of Sudan, low-lying desert terrain dominates the landscape. To the west is the Libyan Desert, the regional name of the eastern Sahara. The arid landscape located east of the Nile Valley is the Nubian Desert. Both are part of the vast desert belt that stretches across northern Africa and into southwestern and central Asia. The desert is dominated by *reg* (gravel), *hamada* (rocky), and *erg* (sandy) surface conditions that vary from place to place.

Northern Sudan is comprised of desert and the Nile Valley. Western Sudan is very dry, thus people and animals must remain in reach of permanent wells, making the population unevenly distributed and sparse. Several mountain ranges in the far south, northeast, and west break up the flat terrain. Sudan is abundant in rich mineral resources including petroleum, natural gas, iron, zinc, gold, and uranium.

In the south, the lowlands are dominated by As Sudd, one of the world's largest wetland areas of marsh (reeds and other aquatic plants) and swamp (standing water and trees). The soggy region covers nearly 100,000 square miles (260,000 sq km), an area about the size of Colorado. Physically, the vast wetlands are formed by periodic flooding of very flat and poorly drained land by the Nile and its tributaries.

Scattered about between the highlands and lowlands are a number of upland areas best described as hills. They include the Nuba Mountains and the Ingessana Hills, the latter being an important chromium-producing area.

WEATHER AND CLIMATE

Sudan's latitudinal location places most of the country within the tropics. Tropical refers to temperature conditions, not moisture. A tropical location is defined as being any place in which the average temperature of the coldest month is above 64.4°F (18°C). There are three topical zones: wet tropics (not found in Sudan), seasonal wet-and-dry tropics, and dry tropics. (Note: Each of these climatic zones is identified by a number of different names and defined by various conditions.) A small area of northern Sudan experiences a dry subtropical climate. There, the average temperature of the coldest month drops below 64.4°F (18°C), but is above freezing. This section describes the most important aspects of both weather (day-to-day conditions of the atmosphere) and climate (long term average weather conditions).

Weather and climate are a mixture of temperature, precipitation, atmospheric pressure, and winds. In various combinations, they create a fifth element—storms. Many factors influence weather and climate. Certainly latitude plays an important role. Sudan's tropical location, for example, is responsible for the country's constantly high temperatures. But among other influences are air masses, pressure systems and winds, elevation, and distance from a large body of water. As you can see, the atmosphere is very complex. In this section, only those elements that are most important to conditions in Sudan are discussed.

In Sudan, precipitation is far and away the most important element of weather and climate. Of particular importance is the amount of rain that falls annually, when rain falls, and the length and severity of the dry season. Many human activities are finely tuned to these seasonal changes in weather. Basically, most of the country experiences either seasonally wet-and-dry conditions, or year-round aridity.

The change between wet and dry seasons is explained by the movement of pressure systems and air masses. (An air mass is a body of air that takes on the conditions of the area over which it forms.) In simple terms, think of the southern part of Sudan as lying between two weather extremes. To the north, in the Sahara Desert, conditions are dry year-round. To the south, along the equator, they are wet throughout the year.

As you probably know, the position of the sun moves northward during the Northern Hemisphere summer and southward during the hemisphere's winter. As it makes its annual migration, the sun "drags" with it Earth's climatic belts and their controls. During the Northern Hemisphere summer, those conditions that contribute to high rainfall all year along the equator move northward. This is southern Sudan's wet season. During the winter months, the sun drags southward the belt of conditions that cause aridity in the Sahara and northern Sudan year-round. This creates the region's dry season.

The northern part of Sudan experiences a desert climate (much of which is dry-tropical) throughout the year. If you have a barometer, what weather conditions are indicated by rising atmospheric pressure? If you answered with words such as *calm, stable, clear,* and *fair,* you are right! High pressure is associated with calm, non-stormy conditions. Most of northern Africa, including northern Sudan, lies in a belt of year-round high pressure. It is this pressure system that contributes to the region's year-round lack of cloud cover and resulting aridity.

Temperature

Temperatures in Sudan vary somewhat from region to region, although no inhabited location experiences extreme cold. (Snow occasionally falls on higher peaks.) Generally speaking, drier locations experience greater temperature extremes than do places with a humid climate and frequent cloud cover. In fact, day-to-night temperature differences, particularly in drier areas, can be greater than annual temperature ranges! In a dry atmosphere, there is little moisture or cloud cover to block incoming solar radiation. This allows daytime temperatures to soar. On the other hand, at night, there is no atmospheric "blanket" to keep heat on or near Earth's surface. In the dry desert atmosphere, daytime temperatures can be sweltering hot, climbing to extremes well above 100°F (37.7°C). Yet during the nighttime they can plummet to teeth chattering temperatures in the 40s (4.4-9.4°C) or even lower.

In Sudan, temperatures do not vary greatly from month to month. The range is greater in the arid north than in the more humid southern part of the country. In Khartoum, Sudan's capital and largest city, the average annual temperature is 80°F (26.7°C). (Phoenix, Arizona, experiences an annual average temperature of 69.2°F [20.67°C].) The warmest months are May and June—just before the onset of the wet season—when afternoon highs average about 106°F (41°C). The city's record high temperature is a sweltering 118° F (48°C)! In January, temperatures in Khartoum average 59° F (15°C), with a record low temperature of only 41° F (5°C).

In the more humid south, annual average temperatures are higher than in the north. Averages in the upper 70s to lower 80s (25 to 28°C) are common. Juba, located near the Ugandan border, experiences conditions typical to the region. The city's average annual temperature is 81.1°F (27.5C). During the warm season the average daily high temperature is in the upper 90s (36-37°C). Daily low temperatures during the cooler season drop to an average 68°F (20°C).

As always seems to be the case, there are some exceptions to the general rules that have been presented here. For example, temperatures can drop well-below freezing at high elevations and snow falls occasionally atop the higher mountains. In the north, an occasional cold front can bring unseasonably cold temperatures. Another seemingly strange condition is that highest temperatures do not happen during the summer (high sun) period. Rather, they occur just before, or at the end of the dry season when cloudless skies allow them to climb. Finally, the south experiences the highest year-round average temperatures, but it lacks the extremely high temperatures that occur in the north.

Precipitation

As you have seen, most of Sudan has an arid to semiarid climate. Only in the far south are conditions quite moist. Such rain occurs mostly during the late spring, summer, and early autumn months. Not all locations, of course, have moisture spread out over half a year. The specific time of year, length of the rainy season, and amount of rainfall vary from place to place. Most rain falls in the form of thundershowers. Because there is little vegetation to slow run-off, rainfall can accumulate rapidly and create flash-flood conditions. The roaring water of a flash flood can wash away everything in its path with devastating ferocity. You may be surprised to know that in desert regions (including the Southwestern U.S.), many more people are killed by flash floods than by dust storms!

In terms of precipitation, Khartoum is typical of northern Sudan. The city has a very light rainy season that lasts from July through September. Total annual average rainfall is about 6 inches (150 millimeters), roughly the same as Phoenix, Arizona. Conditions are considerably wetter in the south. Yambo, a city close to the Democratic Republic of the Congo in far southwestern Sudan, is the country's wettest location. It has a nine-month rainy season (very unique for Sudan!) and averages 44 inches

(1,142 mm) of precipitation a year. This is slightly more than the average for most of southern Sudan. Juba, which is typical of the region, averages about 39 inches (990 mm) of rain annually.

Throughout most of Sudan, an inadequate water supply poses a major problem for settlement and economic develop-ment. Whereas people have learned to adapt to conditions of water scarcity, frequent periods of severe drought can be devas-tating. When gripped by drought, many water supplies vanish, crops wither, livestock die, and extreme hardship stalks the land and its people.

Dust Storms

Summer is the season of the *haboob,* a hot, howling, dusty wind common to the region. The term comes from an Arabic word meaning "strong wind." These storms occur mainly along the southern margins of the Sahara Desert, including northern Sudan. They approach as a dense wall of sand and dust that can reach a height of 3,000 feet (900 m). When they strike, blinding sand and dust can blacken the sky as the darkest night.

Most haboobs form in association with a huge convectional cell (clouds with vertical development and often accompanied by thunderstorms). As a result, the storms can create a double whammy of blown sand and dust followed by drenching rain, or mud storm. Fortunately, the storms usually are of short duration, rarely lasting more than an hour or so. Light dust particles, however, can remain in the sky for days, making the sun look like a copper penny suspended in the heavens. Storms identical to the haboob sometimes occur in the desert regions of North America, Asia, and Australia.

NATURAL VEGETATION

A very close relationship exists between precipitation and natural vegetation cover. Desert landscapes cover about 36 percent of Sudan's area. Here, annual rainfall averages less than 3 inches (125 mm). Plants struggle and those that can survive

A haboob, which means "strong wind" in Arabic, is a gigantic sandstorm commonly seen in arid regions around the world. These seasonal storms can occur at any time without warning, usually lasts about three hours, and can reach a height of about 3,000 feet (900 m). Above, a haboob spreads over Khartoum, Sudan's capital city.

have developed unique ways to get by with minimal moisture. Adaptation takes many forms. Most plants are small and have very deep root systems. Some have small leaves, leaves that turn against the sun during daylight hours, or leaves with waxy coatings. In each case, leaves are designed to reduce transpiration (water loss).

A semidesert belt covers about 20 percent of Sudan. This region receives between 5 and 12 inches (125 to 300 mm) of rainfall annually. Vegetation here is mainly short grass and low scrub. As moisture increases southward, the semidesert belt gives way to a savanna landscape of taller grasses and scattered trees. The region, which covers about 24 percent of the country, receives from 12 to 35 inches (300 to 900 mm) of rainfall a year. Fire is the key to savanna landscapes. During the wet season, plant growth is extensive, but in the dry season, conditions become parched and plants withered. For millennia, the dried vegetation has been burned by people living in savanna environments. This creates an open landscape that favors grasses. The trees that grow here are pyrophytic (fire resistant), such as the gnarly baobab and umbrella-shaped acacias. Under natural conditions, woodlands are found on floodplains, in mountainous areas, and in areas that receive more than 35 inches (900 mm) of rainfall each year. They cover about 8 percent of Sudan's area.

Africa is the world's longest inhabited continent. Over hundreds of thousands of years, human activity has drastically changed the "natural" vegetation. Change has come from the widespread use of fire as a tool for clearing land, cutting wood for various purposes, and, during recent millennia, farming and grazing of livestock.

ANIMAL LIFE

When most people think of Africa's savanna landscapes, what do you think comes to mind? If you said "animals," you are right. Sudan has some of the continent's most varied, abundant, and spectacular wildlife populations. Nearly all of the animals, including some 300 species of mammals, are found in the southern part of the country. There, herbivorous (vegetarian) animals graze on the tall savanna grasses. They, in turn, are preyed upon by carnivorous (meat eating) predators such as lions and hyenas. Finally, vultures and other carrion-eating birds, animals, and insects clean up the mess.

A recent wildlife survey conducted in southern Sudan counted more than 1.2 million antelope of various types. It also counted at least 8,000 elephants, as well as substantial numbers of buffalos, lions, giraffes, and hartebeests. There are also a number of animals adapted to the forest environment. They include several types of monkeys, the bongo antelope, chimpanzees, forest elephants, and at least two types of large wild hogs.

The country is home to more than 200 bird species, including ostriches and storks. Fish and other aquatic species too numerous to mention are found in the Nile and its tributaries. They include hippopotami and huge (and frequently man-eating!) crocodiles. Many species also are found in the waters of the Red Sea. As is true throughout the tropical world, Sudan has more than its share of insects, including many that spread diseases such as malaria. And, oh, yes, we wouldn't want to forget the more than two dozen venomous snakes, animals, and insects and the huge python constrictor!

Sudan's fauna has been threatened for some time. During the decades-long civil war, "bush meat" (wildlife) was a primary source of food for many people. A fortune could be made by poaching elephants for their valuable ivory tusks. Damage to the environment has destroyed animal habitats. Today, many concerned people fear that economic development will further destroy animal habitats, both land and water. Agriculture, mining, and petroleum production all change and pollute the environment. And with the end of civil conflict, all of these activities are increasing. Looking ahead, abundant wildlife offers a safari option to regional economic development. For this to happen, however, peaceful conditions must prevail and an adequate tourist infrastructure must be developed.

SOILS

About 7 percent of Sudan's area is arable, or suitable for farming, but only 0.17 percent of the country's land is actually farmed. Soils, therefore, are of regional importance, but of little significance to the country's economy as a whole. The distribution of soils in an arid land is of little importance if water is not available to irrigate crops. This situation helps to explain why only a fraction of 1 percent of the land is farmed, whereas 7 percent is arable.

Soil is more than just dirt. It consists of sand, silt, or clay and contains both minerals and organic material. Generally speaking, desert soils lack organic content, because there is so little vegetation to convert to humus (organic material in soil). But in the dry desert environment, there is little rainfall to leach (wash away) the mineral content. In many areas of medium rainfall, moisture leaches away the minerals, but abundant plant life and soil microorganisms contribute to high humus content. Most desert soils lack humus. Additionally, in some locations they are high in salt content, which is toxic to most plants.

Alluvial soils are those formed by the deposition of silt from streams. You may have read about the annual flooding of the Nile River in Egypt and the rich soils the floods deposited. The soils were so fertile that farming supported thousands of years of Egyptian high culture. Well, Sudan is upstream (the Nile flows north) on the Nile from Egypt! The country's rivers have deposited rich deposits of alluvium, but there is a problem. In many places, particularly in southern Sudan, areas of alluvial soils are flooded seasonally or throughout the year (as in As Sudd).

Agriculturally, Sudan's most important soils are the "cracking soils" found in scattered locations throughout the central part of the country. They are clays in which large cracks form when they dry out during the dry season, hence, their strange name. When the rains return, the cracks allow water to seep into the soil. Agriculture in the cracking soil belt is both dry land (rain fed) and irrigated. It also is practiced by traditional cultivators growing crops for subsistence, and mechanized commercial farming.

WATER FEATURES

For centuries, the Nile has been Sudan's lifeline just as it has been to Egypt. The river's length is a hotly contested issue. (This is true of many rivers. The problem results from debating the location where a river's most distant tributary actually begins.) Most scholars agree that the Nile is 4,163 miles (6,700 km) long, making it the world's longest river. It has several headwaters. The White Nile flows out of Central Africa's Lake Victoria, where it cascades down Ripon Falls. There, it drains highland regions of Uganda, Rwanda, and Burundi. The Blue Nile flows in a southwesterly direction from Ethiopia's Lake Tana. (If you have difficulty remembering which is the White Nile and which is the Blue Nile, just remember that the White Nile is the westernmost of the two tributaries.) Both headwaters are in the equatorial region of Central Africa where rainfall is heavy. There are, of course, other tributaries that feed into these rivers. Ultimately, the Nile flows into the Mediterranean Sea through its fertile and historically important delta in Egypt. Nearly all of Sudan lies within the drainage basin of the Nile and its two main tributaries, the Blue Nile (Al Bahr al Azraq) and the White Nile (Al Bahr al Abyad).

As Sudd, the great marsh and swamp of the Nile, spreads over much southern Sudan. Here, the White Nile and its tributaries do not follow a well-defined channel. Rather, the water slowly wanders through a maze of lakes and marshes choked with reeds and papyrus. As the water spreads out in the warm tropical environment, a lot of it is lost to evaporation. In 1978, Sudan and France began to build the Jonglei Canal. The ambitious project was supposed to create a channel for the Nile so less water would be lost through evaporation. Also, the canal would improve water transportation through the As Sudd region. Unfortunately, because of Sudan's civil war, the project was discontinued and the canal was never finished.

Only a few of Sudan's streams are not associated with the Nile drainage. In the arid northern desert region, *wadis* (intermittent stream beds that contain water only after a rainstorm) flow into the Red Sea, or simply disappear into small basins or desert sands. Also, some of the rivers flowing into Sudan from Ethiopia flow into shallow, evaporating ponds west of the Red Sea Hills.

Several dams have been built on the White and Blue Nile in Sudan. They are relatively small projects that control the flow

of water, protect against flooding, and provide water for irrigation in some locations. Sudan, however, is home to one mega-
dam project. In 2003, construction began on the Meroe Dam, a
giant structure and hydroelectric installation being built on the
"Great Bend" of the Nile north of Khartoum. Nicknamed the
"Pearl of the Nile," the giant dam will provide water for irrigation and double the country's electricity producing capacity.
The reservoir will extend upstream for nearly 100 miles (160
km). Unfortunately, the man-made lake also will displace more
than 50,000 people. Most experts, however, believe that the
dam, reservoir, and power production will benefit many more
people than it will harm.

The Red Sea provides Sudan with an outlet to global shipping lanes through either Egypt's Suez Canal, or the Strait
of Bab-el-Mandeb that opens into the Indian Ocean. Unfortunately, the country's major port facility, Port Sudan, is far
removed from the centers of population and economic activity.
The sea provides some fishing and also offers great potential for
further development of tourism. In one respect, the Red Sea
stands out: it is the world's saltiest water body that is connected
to the global ocean. Salinity averages 4.1 percent, compared
with the oceanic average of about 3.5 percent. Salt accumulates
in the water for three reasons: first, in the desert region, there
is very little inflow of fresh water; second, the Red Sea is semi-
enclosed and there is little mixing with water of the Indian
Ocean; finally, salts accumulate through time because of the
very high water loss through evaporation.

NATURAL RESOURCES

Sudan has many natural resources. It has woodlands in the south,
widespread grazing lands, and good soils in places. The Nile and
its tributaries provide precious water resources in the otherwise
parched landscapes of central and northern Sudan. The Nile also
offers excellent hydroelectric potential, some of which has been
and is being harnessed. The Red Sea offers fishing, shipping, and

tourism. There is also mineral wealth, including deposits of copper, iron ore, chromium, zinc, tungsten, mica, silver, and gold. Sudan's most important economic resource, by a wide margin, is petroleum. Huge deposits have been discovered—by some estimates, comparable in size to those of the Middle East. The country began to export oil in 1999 and certainly this source of revenue will expand greatly during coming decades.

ENVIRONMENTAL PROBLEMS

Sudan faces a number of serious environmental problems. Warfare, of course, is a major destroyer of environments. Certainly the country's long history of conflict has taken a huge toll on the natural environment, including natural vegetation and wildlife. Population growth, too, has added to the dependence upon various natural elements. Wildlife is hunted for food, soils are overfarmed, grasslands are overgrazed, and woodlands are overcut for firewood. Stream pollution results from many activities. Wells for irrigation deplete ground water reserves, many of which already have gone bone dry. Two things, in particular, stand out as being most severe in terms of Sudan's natural environment: desertification and deforestation.

Desertification

Desertification is defined as the creation of desert conditions by human activities. It is a condition that threatens more than one-third of Earth's surface (including widespread areas of the western interior of the United States and Canada). In Africa, desertification has been particularly destructive in the Sahel region, of which central Sudan is a part. *Sahel* means "shore," and the geographic region is the southern shore (wetter edge) of the vast Sahara Desert. The entire Sahel region experienced a very severe drought that began in the late 1960s and continued at least to the mid-1980s.

Normally, the Sahel region receives an annual average 10 to 20 inches (250 to 500 mm) of rain. For a period of more than two decades, however, a withering drought struck the area. Conditions were so extreme that in some areas, including in Sudan, desert conditions spread southward a distance of about 60 miles (100 km). Some 20 African countries were affected, including 150 million people. According to some estimates, 100,000 to 250,000 people died from lack of food and water. The toll on livestock was much greater, reaching into the millions.

"But," you might ask, "people have lived here for thousands of years and certainly have experienced many periods of severe drought. Why is the problem so great now?" The answer to this question lies in a key word: *human*. As Sudan's human population continues to increase, the dependence of poor people upon nature and its resource also grows. Herd size increases, resulting in the loss of vegetation cover from overgrazing. More marginally productive land is cleared for farming. Crops are needed to feed an increasing number of rural families and growing urban populations. Woodlands and scrublands are cut to provide firewood for cooking and warmth. Each of these land use practices removes vegetation cover, thereby exposing fragile soil to ruin. Remember the haboobs, the fierce dust storms? When land is laid bare, heavy winds pick up soil particles that become the sky-blackening dust associated with the storms. They are one of the most visible results of desertification.

Deforestation

Between 1990 and 2010, Sudan lost nearly 12 percent, or about 35,000 square miles (90,000 sq km) of forest cover. This is an area slightly larger than the state of South Carolina. The loss of woodland continues at an alarming rate. Each year, about 2,000 square miles (5,200 sq km) of forest is cut down, whereas only about 115 square miles (300 sq km) of land is reforested. Drought, overgrazing, and fire also have destroyed several species of grass and other valuable flora. Most of Sudan's people live where vegetation already has been drastically changed. Basically, the more people who live in an area, the less natural vegetation will there be. About 22 percent of all Sudanese live in the south. So it is

Farming, livestock grazing, and the diversion of rivers for human use historically have been among the leading causes of desertification. The lack of water and fertile land has been a major source of conflict between farmers and nomads in Sudan. According to the Institute for Natural Resources in Africa, if current trends of soil degradation continue, Africa will be able to feed only 25 percent of its population by 2025.

not surprising that the area has some two-thirds of the country's remaining forest and tall grass savanna cover.

Historically, the leading causes of deforestation in Sudan—and especially in the troubled Darfur region—have been attributed to overfarming and livestock grazing. This widespread belief has spawned conflicts over which group, farmers or herders, should have claim to the land.

CHAPTER

3

People and Culture

In this chapter, we will take a close look at Sudan's people. First, you will learn about the country's population as you are introduced to key demographic data (population statistics) and their importance. Second, you will find that Sudan is a country with an incredible diversity of ethnic groups. Contrasting ways of life and group identities, as you will see, is both a blessing and a frequent source of conflict. Finally, you will get a glimpse of the most important culture traits of the Sudanese people, including their languages and religions.

It is often suggested that Sudan is Africa in a microcosm. As elsewhere on the huge continent, the country suffers from rapid population growth and a host of other demographic problems. Like the rest of North Africa, it has a strong Arab-Muslim presence, which is in sharp conflict with traditional African peoples. During the colonial era, Sudan (and most of the rest of Africa) was influenced by French, British, and other European powers, each of which left a strong cultural imprint. As a result, most African cultures are a colorful blending of many different ways of life.

POPULATION

In mid-2009, Sudan's population was estimated to be just over 41 million. In 2008, the country conducted its first full census since it gained independence in 1956. (Most demographic data appearing in this chapter are based on U.S. government estimates. For current estimates, see *CIA World Factbook*.) Among African nations, Sudan ranks sixth in population, behind Nigeria, neighboring Ethiopia, Egypt, and the Democratic Republic of the Congo, and South Africa. Because Sudan is Africa's largest country, you might think that it would have more people. But you must remember that much of its area is desert, marsh or swamp, or mountainous. Sudan's population density of 44 people per square mile (17 per sq km) is almost meaningless. In some places, such as in and around Khartoum, the population density is huge. Elsewhere, vast areas support almost no population at all.

Population Change

Four factors determine whether a country's population changes—births, deaths, out-migration, and in-migration. Using these data, there are several ways to measure changes in a country's population. Perhaps the most useful statistic is the rate of natural (population) increase, or RNI. A country's RNI is based upon birth rates and death rates. Between 2008 and 2009, Sudan experienced 33.74 births and 12.94 deaths per 1,000 people, resulting in a 2.08 RNI. This is slightly below the 2.4 percent annual increase for Africa as a whole, but a nearly full percent greater than the 1.2 percent world figure.

You must remember that the RNI is based upon *natural* increase. It reflects population change based upon the balance of births over deaths. When migration is factored in, the country's population is growing by about 2.14 percent annually. As of 2010 and based upon the country's RNI and net migration, Sudan's current population is growing by about 880,000 people a year. By 2025, Sudan's population is expected to increase to around 57 million.

Another way to assess population change is the total fertility rate (TFR), the average number of children to which women give birth during their fecund (fertile) years. For Sudan, the TFR is 4.48, more than double the replacement rate of 2.1. (The 2 is based upon a male and a female; the 0.1 is explained by the fact that some women will never have children.) This is well above the world average of 2.6, but below the figure for most other African countries. Fortunately, the rate of population growth Sudan is dropping gradually. When a country's population growth rate slows, it imposes less of a burden on the economy. The government, for example, is better able to provide services such as education, health care, and infrastructure development. Currently, Sudan's economy is growing at around 6 to 7 percent annually, so it is expanding faster than is the population.

Finally, migration—both in and out—can change a country's population. Currently, Sudan is experiencing a net gain from migration (0.63/1,000), or about 25,800 people each year. As you soon shall see, however, the country's migration patterns fluctuate greatly from year to year. Migration is so important to Sudan that it is discussed separately later in this chapter.

Demographics of Well-Being

Several sets of demographic data can offer valuable clues to the well-being of a country and its people. They include life expectancy, age structure, and infant mortality rate. Life expectancy, the average number of years a person is expected to live at birth, is perhaps the most important index. Average life expectancy in Sudan is 51.4 years, 52.4 for females and 50.5 for males. Among the world's nations, the country ranks a dismal two hundred fourth among the 224 states for which data are available. Sadly, although not surprisingly, 19 of the 20 countries with an even shorter life expectancy are in Africa.

Age structure also can tell us a great deal about the well-being of a country's people. Population pyramids provide a visual breakdown of a nation's population age and sex structure. As is true of most less-developed countries, Sudan's population is quite young. The median (middle) age is 19.1 years and a whopping 41 percent of the population is under 15 years old (versus 20.2 percent for the United States and 12.8 percent for Canada). Decades of warfare, poor diets, inadequate health services, and other factors have taken a dreadful toll on the Sudanese. Only 2.5 percent of them are 65 or older (compared to 16.1 percent of Americans and 15.2 percent of Canadians).

One of the most valid indicators of a country's standard of living is its infant mortality rate, the number of deaths per 1,000 from birth to age one year. Sudan experiences a horrendous loss of 82 deaths per 1,000 live births during the first year. This is nearly twice as high as the world average of 46/1,000. (In the economically developed world, figures are comparable to those of the United States and Canada, 6.6/1,000 and 5.0/1,000, respectively.) Infant mortality may be the best indicator of a country's medical care, health services, sanitation and hygiene, nutrition, and other health conditions. Obviously, they are lacking throughout much of Sudan.

Considerable geographic variations exist in data that relate to human well-being. According to the United Nations Children's Fund (UNICEF), death rates among people who have been forced to flee their homes in Darfur are up to 10 times higher than those for the rest of Sudan's population. In overcrowded camps with little clean water and poor sanitary conditions, infant mortality rates soar. Throughout Sudan, diarrhea is the cause of death for 3 out of every 4 children who die before age five. Moreover, while 50 percent of Sudan's urban population had adequate sanitation facilities in 2004, only 24 percent of the rural population had this sort of access.

HUMAN DEVELOPMENT

As you have seen, population information can tell us more than just numbers. The United Nations has developed a system for measuring human development. Its Human Development Index (HDI) is a comparative measure of living standards, life expectancy, education, literacy, and other measures. Using this yardstick, Sudan ranks 150 among the 182 countries included in the survey. As bad as this may look, among African's 54 countries, Sudan is not that bad off. Only eight African nations rank higher than Sudan on the HDI. Despite this high standing on the continent, the country has a very long way to go before its people enjoy a standard of living comparable to that of the world's developed lands.

One huge challenge facing Sudan's government is that of educating its people. Only about 60 percent of the population can read and write and only half of the country's females are literate. Until its citizens become better educated, Sudan faces an up-hill struggle in improving the country's economy and social development.

MIGRATION

Why do people migrate, or move from place to place? Geographers explain migration by using a simple push-and-pull model. Many places have positive attractions that draw people to that location. They are called pull forces. In traditional societies, better hunting, fishing, and gathering opportunities, or more or better land on which to farm or graze livestock may pull people to a new location. Today, when most people move, they are pulled to places that offer a better economic opportunity, such as a job, a higher salary, or greater employment security. For some people, good schools, quality health and medical facilities, environmental amenities such as a good climate, and even low housing costs can be a draw.

At the same time, many places have certain negative characteristics, or push forces, that influence people leaving that location. Examples of push forces include poor economic opportunities, such as unemployment or low salaries. Environmental conditions such as drought, land shortage, and social unrest can push people from a place. Some factors are completely neutral. For example, if someone is retired, then employment opportunities will not be a deciding factor in whether to move (push) or where to migrate (pull). Some moves are strictly voluntary, although people generally do move to locations with desirable pull factors. The scenarios described above are all examples of voluntary migration. People move freely, at the time they choose and after considering their alternatives with the best information available, to the destination of their choice.

Not all migration is voluntary. In fact, a considerable amount of migration is involuntary. Sometimes, migrants have no choice over the timing, the destination, or the mode of transport used for the move. They are transported against their will. Slaves brought to the Americas from West Africa were not voluntary migrants. Slavery is an excellent example of forced migration.

Yet another migration category is displaced people. In this case, people may be reluctant to move, but are compelled to relocate by circumstances beyond their control, such as famine, war, drought, or persecution. They are forced to move because they feel threatened in some way. This is the case with internally displaced people. Fleeing war, religious or political persecution, or some other negative condition, they move to a place that offers peace and refuge. In Sudan, for example, an estimated 500,000 southern Sudanese, have left their poor and troubled homeland and moved to North Sudan.

When displaced people cross an international boundary, the United Nations High Commission for Refugees (UNHCR) calls them refugees. Thus, areas close to ongoing conflict usually have large numbers of people who have fled their homes in order to move to a safer place. Similarly, countries adjoining war-torn places have large numbers of refugees. This is the situation with Sudan and its neighbors.

SUDANESE REFUGEES

An unknown number of Sudanese have left their country for a variety of reasons. A substantial number of them have become refugees in other lands. In 2009, Chad, Ethiopia, Kenya, Central African Republic, the Democratic Republic of the Congo, and Uganda all provided shelter for hundreds of thousands of Sudanese refugees. Eastern Chad alone provided a temporary home to about 250,000 refugees who had fled the conflict in Sudan's Darfur region.

Sudan's almost constant wars also have affected all of its neighboring countries. Even though Sudan generates its own refugees that flee elsewhere, the country also is a host to large numbers of refugees. According to the *World Refugee Survey 2008*, published by the U.S. Committee for Refugees and Immigrants, 310,500 refugees and asylum seekers lived in Sudan in 2007. Most of them came from neighboring countries of Eritrea, Chad, Ethiopia, and the Central African Republic.

Whether internally displaced, or in a foreign country, refugees face similar difficulties. They are usually victims of violence, rape, unwanted pregnancies, and physical and mental torture. They also have huge unmet health needs. For example, women and girls who fled the fighting in Darfur faced rape and other violence in eastern Chad. This is true even inside the refugee camps where they have sought sanctuary. Amnesty International reports attacks by villagers living nearby, members of Chad's army, and even aid workers in the camps. They are especially vulnerable when they venture outside refugee camps to collect firewood or water.

Around 200,000 Sudanese refugees from Darfur have fled to neighboring Chad to live in United Nations refugee camps, and more than 100,000 Chadian villagers have fled their own villages to live in the camps. Twelve camps in the region house 250,000 Sudanese who have fled the area and are now caught in the middle of warring armies.

SETTLEMENT

If allowed to freely choose, people, through time, will settle in those areas where they can make a living. The well-being of a human population depends upon many things. One of the most important is economic development. In some lands, such as much of rural Sudan, well-being depends upon how well people can provide for themselves. Usually, this means they can grow and raise enough food to feed their families and provide themselves with life's other necessities, such as a home, water, and firewood. For most urban societies, provision is different. Urban people depend upon jobs or other ways of surviving in a cash economy where goods and services must be purchased. In Sudan, we find both groups.

Sixty-two percent of Sudanese live in rural environments, leaving only 38 percent residing in urban centers. This is well below the world average, which today is equally divided between rural and urban. A detailed population distribution map of Sudan is quite revealing. It shows, for example, some areas of very dense settlement. About 5 million Sudanese live in Khartoum and surrounding communities. The Nile River satisfies many needs, including domestic use and irrigation. Consequently, about 35 percent of the population lives along the Nile. Towns around the Nile have been the main centers of urban development since the beginning of human settlement in the region. Elsewhere, troubled Darfur has about 7.5 million people and South Sudan an estimated 8.2 million. Most of the desert north supports very few people. Settlements are small and widely scattered, with most developed around oasis sites where water is available.

ETHNIC GROUPS

Few countries can match Sudan's ethnic diversity. At one time, the country was home to an estimated 600 different ethnicities. (There is little agreement on the definition of ethnicity. Here, it is defined as a group of people who share a common racial and cultural heritage, have strong historical ties, and possess a strong feeling of group or self-identity.) At the broadest division, Sudan's population is about 52 percent black, 39 percent Arab, and 6 percent Beja (a traditional culture in eastern Sudan). Additionally, about 3 percent of the population is foreign or "other."

You must remember that for millennia, most Sudanese people lived in small tribal groups. Each such group had its own heritage and sense of being different (often including its language) than others. During recent decades, some of the country's smaller ethnic groups (and languages) have vanished. Some were absorbed by conquest. Others became gradually absorbed into the culture of neighboring ethnic groups. Still others migrated to cities or elsewhere and became acculturated (the process of gradually accepting traits of another culture) into the host's way of life.

Today, as you will see in subsequent chapters, prejudices and discrimination based upon ethnicity continue to be a source of heated conflict in Sudan. Particularly sharp and contentious is the ethnic divide between North and South Sudanese. The differences are racial and cultural, the latter involving language, religion, and other differences.

LANGUAGES

Historically, Sudan has been one of the most ethnically and linguistically diverse countries in the world. At one time, it had nearly 600 ethnic groups speaking more than 400 languages and dialects. In the 1980s and 1990s some of Sudan's smaller ethnic and linguistic groups disappeared. Migration played a part, as migrants often forget their native tongue when they move to an area dominated by another language. Some linguistic groups were absorbed by the process of acculturation (gradually accepting traits of another culture); others were absorbed by conquest.

Today, more than 100 different languages are spoken in Sudan, including Nubian, Ta Bedawie, and dialects of the Nilotic and Nilo-Hamitic languages. Arabic is the country's official language, and is spoken by more than half of the population. English is widely spoken by the educated and elite, particularly those with business or other "global" interests. Nevertheless, English is being phased out as a foreign language taught in the southern schools in an attempt to "Arabicize" the region.

RELIGION

Religion is central to the lives of Sudanese people. Most of the country's most bitter conflicts are related to religious differences. Of the entire Sudanese population, 70 percent is Sunni

Muslim, 25 percent follow traditional indigenous beliefs, and 5 percent are Christian.

Before the arrival of Christianity and Islam, the Sudanese worshipped deities (ancestral spirits) and believed that all living and non-living objects had a soul. Today these religions have changed considerably and embrace many practices from Islam and Christianity. Many Sudanese still honor their dead ancestors to avoid their curses and other sanctions. Shamans (spiritual leaders who are believed to hold special powers) and priests are very common. These religious leaders are believed to have a deep understanding of the spirit world. Often gifts will be presented to the priest to offer to the spirits in order to secure blessings.

Islam in Sudan

Both black Africans and Arabs alike practice Islamic traditions. The Muslim peoples of Sudan include the Fur, the Nubians, Beja, Berti, Zaghawa, Masalit, Daju, the Nuba (from the northern side of the Nuba Mountains), and West Africans who live in Sudan. While Sudanese practice Islam in their own ways, in many respects, Islam in itself is a way of life. Therefore, those who practice Islam will experience it in many other aspects of their culture besides in their religion.

The word *Islam* means "submission to God." Islam shares certain prophets, traditions, and beliefs with Judaism and Christianity. The main difference between Islam and these other two faiths is that Muslims believe that Muhammad is the final prophet and the embodiment of God, or Allah.

The foundation of Islamic belief is called the Five Pillars. The first, *Shahada*, is profession of faith. The second is prayer, or *Salat*. Muslims pray five times a day, always toward the holy city of Mecca, in Saudi Arabia. It is not necessary to go to the mosque to do so; the call to prayer echoes out over each city or town from the minarets (towers) of the holy buildings,

Islam is the largest religion in Sudan, with the remainder of the population following Christianity or traditional animist religion. Northern Muslims have ruled political and economic institutions since Sudan achieved its independence in 1956, which has led to major conflicts in the country. Above, Muslims in Darfur listen to the local imam in the Muhajariah mosque.

calling people to prayer. The third pillar, *Zakat*, is the principle of giving money to the poor. The fourth is fasting, which is observed during the month of Ramadan each year. (The timing of Ramadan follows the Islamic calendar, which is different than the Western calendar. Therefore, the month of Ramadan takes place at a different time in the Western calendar each year.) During Ramadan, Muslims abstain from food and drink, among other activities, during the daylight hours. The fifth pillar is the *Hajj*, the pilgrimage to the holy city of Mecca, which all able Muslims must make at some time in their life.

All Muslims are required to respect the Five Pillars of Islam, although it is common that many do not. It is more likely that a Muslim who lives in an urban setting will pray at the prescribed times. The consistent observance of prayer is the mark of a true Muslim.

There are no priests in Islam. *Fakis* and *sheiks* are holy men who dedicate themselves to the study and teaching of the Koran, Islam's holy book. The Koran, rather than any religious leader, is considered to be the ultimate authority, and is believed to hold the answer to any question or dilemma one might have. *Muezzins* give the call to prayer and also are scholars of the Koran.

The most important observation in the Islamic calendar is that of Ramadan. This month of fasting is followed by the joyous feast of Eid ul-Fitr, during which families visit and exchange gifts (much like Christmas in the Christian world). The celebration known as Eid al-Adha commemorates the end of Muhammad's Hajj. Other celebrations include the return of a pilgrim from Mecca and the circumcision of a child.

Weddings also involve important and elaborate rituals, including hundreds of guests and several days of celebration. The festivities begin with the henna night, when the groom's hands and feet are dyed. This is followed the next day with the bride's preparation, in which all of her body hair is removed and she, too, is decorated with henna. She also takes a smoke bath to perfume her body. The religious ceremony is relatively simple; in fact, the bride and groom themselves are often not present, but are represented by male relatives who sign the marriage contract for them. Festivities may continue for several days. On the third morning, the bride's and groom's hands are tied together with silk thread, signifying their union.

The mosque is the Muslim house of worship. Outside the door there are washing facilities, as cleanliness is necessary before prayer, because it demonstrates humility before God. One also must remove one's shoes before entering the mosque.

According to Islamic tradition, women are not allowed inside these holy buildings. The interior has no altar; it is simply an open carpeted space. Because Muslims are supposed to pray facing Mecca, there is a small niche carved into the wall that points out in which direction the city lies. (Sudanese, for example, pray toward the northeast.) Among the Dinka and other Nilotic cattle herding peoples, cattle sheds serve as shrines and gathering places.

Greetings are interactions with religious overtones. The common expressions all have references to Allah, which are taken not just metaphorically but also literally. *Insha Allah* ("if Allah wills") is often heard, as is *alhamdu lillah* ("may Allah be praised").

Death and the Afterlife

In the Muslim tradition, death is followed by several days of mourning when friends, relatives, and neighbors pay their respects to the family. Female relatives of the deceased wear black for several months to a year or more after the death. Widows generally do not remarry, and they often dress in mourning clothes for the rest of their lives. Like most Christians, Muslims believe in an afterlife. They believe in a day of judgment in which the body and soul will be assigned to an eternal destination—a "paradise" or "hell."

Other Practices

When a child is born, the father will whisper the *adhaan*, or call to prayer, and the name *Allah* in the right ear of the baby. In traditional practice, after seven days of the child's birth, the baby's hair will be shaved off and its weight in gold will be given to charity. The name of the child is also chosen on the seventh day.

OTHER RELIGIONS IN SUDAN

The religion of the indigenous people, or the original people, is animist. This means that people believe in spirits who live in natural objects such as trees, rivers, rocks, and also animals. Often an individual clan will have its own totem (an object believe to be sacred), which represents the clan's first ancestor. The spirits of ancestors are worshiped and believed to exercise an influence in everyday life. There are multiple gods who serve different purposes. Specific beliefs and practices vary widely from tribe to tribe and from region to region. Certain cattle-herding tribes in the south place great symbolic and spiritual value on cows, which sometimes are sacrificed in religious rituals.

Many indigenous ceremonies focus on agricultural events. Two of the most important occasions are the rainmaking ceremony, to encourage a good growing season, and the harvest festival, after the crops are brought in.

Christianity is practiced by only 5 percent of the Sudanese population. Denominations active within Sudan include the Roman Catholics, Episcopalians, Coptic Christians, Presbyterians, and Sudanese Pentecostals. Other Christian groups include the Africa Inland Church, Greek Orthodox, Seventh Day Adventists, the Sudanese Church of Christ, and the Evangelical Church. The Jehovah's Witnesses are also present.

Christianity is most common among the southern Nilotic peoples, the Madi, Moru, Azande, and Bari. Both Christianity and the indigenous religions are more concentrated in the south. This is partly because during the colonial period, British law forbade missionaries and all peoples living in the south to go northward beyond 10° North latitude, so they concentrated their efforts in the south (people living in the north were also forbidden to travel south). Most of the Christians are of the wealthier, educated class, as much of the conversion is done through the schools. Many Sudanese, regardless of religion, hold certain superstitions, such as belief in the evil eye. The evil eye, according to believers, can cause harm or bad luck on the person to whom it is directed. This term has been around for about 1,000 years among many cultures, particularly in the Middle East, East and West Africa, South Asia, Central Asia, and the Mediterranean region in Europe. It is common to wear an amulet or a charm as protection against its powers.

TRADITIONAL PRACTICES

The Sudanese have many different cultural practices, thereby making it very difficult to generalize practices for the whole country. For each practice discussed, there are exceptions—in some cases, many. What follows is a list of the ways in which the majority of people conduct their activities.

Marriage

In traditional tribal society, the parents of a couple traditionally arrange the couple's marriage. This is still the case today, even among wealthier and more-educated Sudanese. Matches are often made between cousins, second cousins, or other family members, or if not, at least between members of the same tribe and social class. Parents conduct the negotiations, and it is common for a bride and groom not to have seen each other before the wedding. There is generally a significant age difference between husband and wife. A man must be economically self-sufficient and able to provide for a family before he can marry. He has to be able to furnish an acceptable bride price of jewelry, clothes, furniture, and, among some tribes, cattle. Among the middle class, women usually are married after they finish school, at age 19 or 20. In poorer families and in rural areas, the marriage age usually is younger. Polygamy (a man having multiple wives) was a common practice in the past. Divorce, although still considered shameful, is more common today than it once was. Upon termination of a marriage, the bride price is returned to the husband.

Extended families often live together under the same roof, or at least nearby. Husband and wife typically move in with the wife's family for at least a year after marriage. After their first child is born, they may move elsewhere, although usually to a house close to the wife's parents.

Inheritance

Islamic law states that the oldest male son inherits his father's wealth. Other inheritance traditions vary from tribe to tribe. In the north, among the Arab population, property goes to the eldest son. Among the Azande, a man's property (which consists primarily of agricultural goods) was generally destroyed upon his death to prevent the accumulation of wealth. Among the Fur, property is usually sold upon the death of its owner. In this tribe, land is owned jointly by kin groups and therefore not divided upon death.

Kin Groups

In various regions of Sudan, traditional clan structures function differently. In some regions, one clan holds all positions of leadership; in others, authority is spread among various clans and sub-clans. Kinship ties are drawn through connections on both the mother's and the father's side, although the paternal (father's) line is given stronger consideration.

Infant Care and Child Rearing

There are several religious practices to protect newborn babies. For example, Muslims whisper Allah's name in the baby's right ear, and Christians make the sign of the cross in water on his or her forehead. An indigenous tradition is to tie an amulet or a fish bone from the Nile around the child's neck or arm.

Women carry their babies tied to their sides or backs with cloth. They often bring them along to work in the fields. Boys and girls are raised fairly separately. Both are divided into age-specific groups. There are celebrations to mark a group's graduation from one life stage to the next. For boys, the transition from childhood to manhood is marked by a circumcision ceremony.

Education

The literacy rate—the number of people who can read and write—in Sudan is only 46 percent overall (58 percent for men and 36 percent for women), but the overall education level of the population has increased since independence. In the mid-1950s, fewer than 150,000 children were enrolled in primary school, compared with more than 2 million today. Christian missionaries established most of the schools in the south during colonial times, but the government closed those schools in 1962. Today the south has fewer schools than the north.

In villages, children usually attend Islamic schools known as *khalwa*. They learn to read and write, to memorize parts of the Koran, and to become members of an Islamic community. Boys usually attend the khalwa between ages 5 and 19. Typically, girls receive less education than boys, as families often consider it more valuable for their daughters to learn domestic skills and to work at home. As payment at the khalwa, students or their parents contribute labor or gifts to the school. There also is a state-run school system, which includes six years of primary school, three years of secondary school, and either a three-year college preparatory program or four years of vocational training.

Early in the twentieth century, under Anglo-Egyptian rule, the only educational institution beyond the primary level was Grodon Memorial College, established in 1902 in Khartoum. The original buildings of this school are today part of the University of Khartoum, which was founded in 1956. The Kitchener School of Medicine (opened in 1924), the School of Law, and the Schools of Agriculture, Veterinary Science, and Engineering are all part of the university. The capital city alone has three universities. There also is one in Wad Medani and another in the southern city of Juba. The first teacher training school, Bakht er Ruda, opened in 1934 in the small town of Ed Dueim. In addition, a number of technical and vocational schools throughout the country

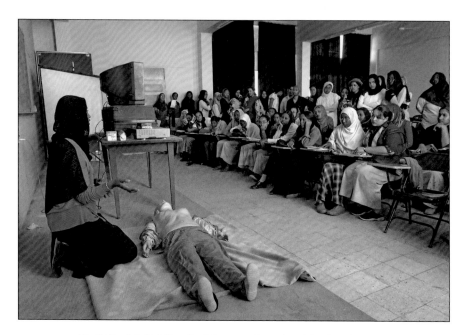

Until Sheikh Babiker Badri opened a school for his daughters in his house in 1907, girls were not allowed to attend school or could only go to the khalwa (religious school). Today his school is now the biggest university for women in Sudan, called Ahfad University for Women. Above, a class learns cardiopulmonary resuscitation at the Faculty of Nursing at Ahfad University.

offer training in nursing, agriculture, and other skilled professions. Ahfad University College, which opened in 1920 in Omdurman as a girls' primary school, has done a great deal to promote women's education and currently enrolls about 1,800 female students.

Food and Dining

Food is an important part of many social interactions. Visits to a person's home typically include tea, coffee, or soda, if not a full meal. It is customary to eat from a common serving bowl, using the right hand (which is used in all "clean" activities), rather than utensils. In Muslim households, people sit on pillows around a low table. Before the meal, towels and a pitcher of water are passed around for hand washing.

The ritual of hospitality is as important in Sudan as it is in other Arab and African countries. Although there is a measure of similarity in all the Arab and North African countries, each has its unique characteristics. For example, no other country prepares coffee as the Sudanese do, and if this country has acquired culinary fame, it is for its "Jebena Sudanese." For this drink, the Sudanese fry their coffee beans in a special pot over charcoal and then grind it with cloves and certain spices. They steep it in hot water and serve it lovingly in tiny coffee cups after straining it through a special thresh grass sieve.

In Sudan, if you are an important guest, a sheep will be slaughtered in your honor. Many dishes will then be prepared, each more delicious than the last. Favorite meats are lamb and chicken, and rice is the staple starch. Breads include the Arabian khubz, and the Sudanese also make Kisra, an omelette-like pancake that is part of the Sudanese dinner. Vegetables, raw and cooked, are of infinite variety. Okra (which came to the United States from Africa) is an important ingredient in Bamia-Bamia, an okra lamb stew. Maschi, a triple tomato dish stuffed with beef, is a fun recipe to make.

As in most Arab countries, fruits are peeled and cut in small slices for dessert, but the Sudanese also love sweets. Every housewife knows how to make Creme Caramela (Sudanese caramel custard). Other popular favorites are their unusual teas, which can be made quite simply.

Now it is your turn! Do you want the true taste of Sudan? Here are a few recipes to try at home:

Salatet Zabady Bil Ajur (Cucumber-Yogurt Salad)
This is a delightful, refreshing summer salad that is also popular in Egypt, Turkey, and the Balkans.

Ingredients:
- 2 cups plain yogurt
- 1 clove garlic, finely minced
- 1 large cucumber, peeled, seeded, and shredded or finely diced
- salt and freshly ground pepper

Method:

In a bowl, combine all the ingredients; cover and refrigerate for two to four hours. At serving time, taste and adjust the seasoning, and then serve immediately.

Koftah (Ground Meat Balls; serves 8–10)

Ingredients:
- 2 lb beef
- 2 onions
- 1 slice soft bread
- salt and pepper to taste

Method:

Mince beef and onions until they reach a smooth consistency. Soak bread in water and add to meat, together with the seasoning. Mix well and shape into rounds 2 to 3 inches (5 to 7.5 cm) in diameter. Grill or fry on skewers or in a double grill until cooked.

Cinnamon Tea

Prepare English tea according to package directions (use loose tea). Tea should be infused until it is a bright orange color. Upon serving, place pieces of a cinnamon stick in small teacups and pour hot tea over the cinnamon. Serve with lump sugar.

Holidays

The Sudanese celebrate both Christian and Muslim holidays. During Eid al-Adha (Festival of the Great Sacrifice), it is customary for a family to slaughter a sheep and donate most of the meat to needy families. After the month-long fast of Ramadan, Muslims celebrate Eid ul-Fitr (Breaking of the Fast) with a large get-together of family and friends. On the day of Eid, Zakat (which means "the sharing of wealth") is collected from all those able to donate. The Zakat is then distributed to the poor. Usually Muslims will wear new clothing on the day of Eid to celebrate a fresh, new beginning. The birthday of the Prophet Muhammad is mostly celebrated by children with sweets and cakes.

In southern Sudan, the Christmas holiday starts on December 23 and ends January 15. Christians gather together in church to celebrate Jesus's birth throughout the night, starting at midnight on Christmas Eve. On Christmas Day, people celebrate with singing, dancing, and playing drums. Friends and relatives visit each other and share food, drink, clothes, and stories. Unlike Christmas in the Western world, Christians in Sudan do not celebrate with a Christmas tree, and some may not even know who Santa Claus is.

SUDANESE ART

Silverwork, ivory carving, and leatherwork are most commonly practiced by artists in the north, while wood carving is more common in the south. Music among Muslim groups mainly involves Koran recitations. Sudan's dancers known as "whirling dervishes" are famed throughout the world for their spellbinding dances, in which they are accompanied by rhythmic drumming, as they gradually work themselves into a trance. Dervishes are Muslim devotees.

Indigenous Sudanese music involves drums and complex rhythms. Such traditional practices as *zur* (exorcisms) involve drums and rattling instruments. Many Muslims argue that music is forbidden by Islam, while many other Muslims say that the Koran mentions no restrictions on music. When Sharia (Islamic law) was introduced to Sudan in 1989, however, many poets and musicians were imprisoned.

Football, called soccer in the United States, is the most popular sport in Sudan. The Sudan national football team is the Sokoor al-Jediane, or Desert Hawks. The Desert Hawks won the African Cup of Nations in 1970, but have not been as successful since.

SPORTS

Several Sudanese-born basketball players have played in the U.S. National Basketball Association (NBA). These include Deng Gai, Luol Deng, and Manute Bol. Hurdler Todd Matthews-Jouda switched nationalities from American to Sudanese in September 2003 and competed at the 2004 Olympics for Sudan.

Football (soccer), however, is the most popular sport. The Khartoum state league, which began in the late 1920s, is considered to be the oldest soccer league in the whole of Africa. The Sudan Football Association started in 1954. Sokoor al-Jediane (which means "Desert Hawks") is Sudan's national football team. Controlled by the Sudan Football Association, it is one of three teams (the others being Egypt and Ethiopia) to have played in the first African Nations Cup in 1957. In 1970, Sudan hosted the competition, and the national team won the competition.

CENTRIPETAL AND CENTRIFUGAL FORCES IN SUDAN

Geographers define a people with a common language, history, ethnic background, and strong sense of group identity as a *nation*. Thus, the Arab and Muslim northern people comprise a nation. Similarly, the non-Muslim south constitutes another nation. A *state*, on the other hand, is an independent political body with a well-defined territory. States with multiple nations are called *multi-nation states*. Those nations that are divided by political boundaries are called *multi-state nations*. For example, the Sudanese Arabs are a multi-state nation, because they are separated by the Egypt-Sudan boundary. A state with only one nation is called a *nation-state*. True nation states are rare. Japan may be one example.

A common language, religion, and cultural heritage act like a binding force, a glue that unifies people. Geographers call such cultural magnets *centripetal* forces. In contrast, *centrifugal* forces divide people. Multiple languages and religious differences are important centrifugal forces, but can also be centripetal forces. In Sudan, the northerners are divided from the Sudanese people who practice different religions in the south. Thus, conflict between Christians and Muslims, especially over Sharia law, is a major cause of turmoil in Sudan. (Religious differences are also an important reason for political instability in Nigeria, where the southern part is mostly Christian and the northern part is mostly Muslim.)

Generally, a common enemy, a national sports team, national anthems and other symbols, and general satisfaction with the government are centripetal forces. Centripetal forces promote nationalism as people take pride in identifying with the state. In contrast, centrifugal forces cause division and may lead to a breakup of the state, as people identify more with ethnic or regional groups instead of their country.

Frequently, regional groups demand more autonomy (self-rule) from the central government. Such pressures can cause civil war, or the central government might transfer power to such regional groups.

Sudan has numerous centrifugal forces—religion, language, and a northern-based government that some citizens believe to be out of touch and insensitive to southern needs and aspirations. Perhaps the one significant centrifugal force is the Sudanese national soccer team. When the Sokoor al-Jediane are playing, Sudan is one united nation.

Sudan is thus an intriguing example of a multi-nation state. The ongoing crisis in Darfur is practical evidence of the strength of centrifugal forces. The future of Sudan depends on how effectively these tensions are resolved or managed, and how the Sudanese government promotes and celebrates centripetal forces.

4

History
and Politics

S udan has a long and turbulent history. In this chapter, history and politics are combined. Whether discussing early empires, the colonial era, or developments in Sudan since it gained independence in 1956, government and politics have played a key role in determining the country's history.

ANCIENT HISTORY

Few countries in the world can match Sudan in terms of its human history. Archaeologists (scientists who study earlier peoples and culture) believe that humankind originated in equatorial eastern Africa. How long ago this occurred is subject to heated debate, and really is not that important as far as we are concerned here. What is known is that humans (*Homo* species) have been around a very long time. There is evidence that ancient peoples were able to move out of Africa and into Eurasia more than one million years ago. Their route northward almost certainly followed either the Nile River or the coast of the Indian Ocean. Either way, they would have passed through territory that is now Sudan. Unfortunately, regardless of the route traveled, any record of their presence would have disappeared long ago.

Sudan's archaeological record dates back about 60,000 years. Details become clearer the more recent the evidence. For example, a burial site in northern Sudan dated to around 13,000 years ago may offer evidence of the world's earliest documented warfare. Nine thousand years ago, people were engaged in early agricultural pursuits, growing grain and herding cattle, while continuing to hunt and fish the waters of the Nile. With improved sources of food, they were able to settle down in villages. Farming and village life are the foundations upon which early empires were built.

EARLY EMPIRES

Sudan has for much of its history been influenced by its neighbors. Strongest cultural ties are with its northern neighbor, Egypt. But various cultural influences also have come from the Arabian Peninsula (such as Islam and the Arabic language), as well as Chad, the Congo, and Ethiopia, its neighbors to the south. Distant influences also are evident. For example, coastal Sudan has long been exposed to distant lands through its opening on the Red Sea. It also benefitted from cultural exchanges and commerce due to its position at the eastern end of a great trade route that stretched westward along the open savannah south of the Sahara. Goods transported in both directions came from many sources and generated tremendous wealth among early North African empires. (Archaeologists have found artifacts from as far away as China in Timbuktu, one of the locations involved in the early sub-Saharan trade.)

What is now northern Sudan was in ancient times the home of a major kingdom, or, should we say, kingdoms. Actually, it is

Archaeologists have proven that Nubia, an area in northern Sudan, had a settled culture in ancient times. Artifacts such as astronomical devices, rock reliefs, statues, pyramids, and written records have been found in what is called the homeland of one of Africa's earliest black civilizations. Early depictions of Nubians show them having gold-hooped earrings, dark skin, and braided hair, like these statues of Nubian soldiers found in Egypt.

best to think in terms of a high level of culture that flourished for several thousand years, from about 2700 B.C. to around 350 A.D. The kingdom was centered on the upper Nile River basin in an area that stretched from near present-day Khartoum into southern Egypt. Control changed from time to time, as did the name of the kingdom. The site of the center of power also shifted occasionally. In Chapter 2, you read about the Kingdom of Kush and its base near the hill named Jebel Barkal, located along the Nile River north of Khartoum. Around 600 B.C., the center of power shifted to Meroe. Today, a number of pyramids and other structures stand as evidence of the long vanished kingdom.

THE COMING OF CHRISTIANITY AND ISLAM

Religion is one of the most fundamental of all culture traits. Faith can tie people together with a common bond, or be a source of bitter conflict that drives them apart. As you will see in various contexts throughout this book, within Sudan religion has exerted both influences on the country's people. Missionaries brought Christianity to the region in the sixth century and were very successful in converting a large part of the population. By the seventh century a new faith, Islam, emerged in the Arabian Peninsula. It began to spread like wildfire, sweeping into and across North Africa, including Sudan where it soon replaced Christianity. Muslims also introduced many other traits including their language, Arabic, and Sharia law.

STEPS TOWARD INDEPENDENCE

In 1882, Great Britain occupied Egypt and by 1898 had extended its rule southward to include Sudan. Until 1955, Sudan was ruled by the British as the Anglo-Egyptian Sudan. Almost from the beginning, many Sudanese disliked this arrangement. By the dawn of the twentieth century, flames of nationalism were being stoked by a growing cry for independence.

At the same time, Sudan was experiencing a strong north-south polarization of ethnic, religious, and other cultural differences. Up until this time, the British had kept north and south Sudan separate, developing the fertile lands around the Nile Valley in the north, while neglecting the south, east, and Darfur to the west. Consequently, northern Sudan was well educated, mostly Arabic speaking, and Muslim, and had solid political and economic infrastructures. In contrast, southern Sudan was home to mainly poorly educated Christian and animist African groups. And the region was geographically isolated from the rest of the country, economically underdeveloped, and politically powerless.

In order to unite northern and southern Sudan into one political unit for independence, Great Britain organized the Juba Conference in 1947. The conference agreed that northern and southern Sudan should form one state, with one legislative assembly for the entire colony. Subsequently, however, southern Sudanese representatives were largely excluded from the political process and discussions to determine the future of the modern state of Sudan. When the British realized they could not relieve the growing tensions between the north and the south, they reluctantly granted Sudan independence. On January 1, 1956, the British handed political power over to a minority of northern Arab-Muslim elites (who historically had closer ties to Egypt).

Southern leaders agreed to go along with independence, but they insisted that parliament must keep its promise of seriously considering a federal constitution that would allow southerners to be recognized as a secular state with shared power. In a federal state, such as the United States, much if not most power rests with the political sub-divisions (such as states), rather than the central government. If Sudan were a federal state, that would enable other cultures and languages to flourish alongside Islam and Arabic.

After independence, northern politicians immediately opposed federalism (in which power is shared between national and state governments). They argued that it would lead to separation. The politicians in the south began to establish alliances with the other underdeveloped regions of the south in support of federalism. The Federal Party thus formed, which opposed the first post-independence elections in 1957. A transitional constitution was written by politicians in the north, stating that Islam was to be the official religion of the state, Arabic would be the official language, and Sharia one of its main sources of law. Southerners were outraged and unamimously rejected it. This, however, was just the beginning of Sudan's seemingly endless political troubles.

MILITARY RULE UNDER GENERAL ABBOUD (1958–1964)

In 1958, northern miltary leaders led by General Ibrahim Abboud took control of the Sudanese government in a blood-less coup (forced overthrow of a government). General Abboud was determined to "Arabize and Islamize" the south. Conversions to Islam were encouraged. Christian missionaries were severely restricted in activity and, in 1964, they were thrown out of the country entirely. The military began to burn opposition villages, and a number of senior political figures and students fled to the "bush" to join other mutineers of the Sudan African Nationalist Union. The civil war between the north and the south began at this time, in 1962. Due to the poor economic policies and harsh repression of political opponents, General Abboud was ousted during a general strike called the October Revolution of 1964. A transition government, led by Sirr al-Khatim al-Khalifa, oversaw elections that led to a civilian coalition government headed by Muhammad Ahmad Mahjub. The coalition collapsed two years later.

SADIQ AL-MAHDI AND THE ISLAMIC CONSTITUTION (1966–1969)

Sadiq al-Mahdi, a northerner and devout member of the Sufi sect of Islam, became prime minister in 1966. He prompted democracy and political Islam. When Sadiq al-Mahdi took over leadership, he and his followers formed a group, or parliamentary bloc, called the New Forces Congress (NFC). The NFC was comprised of al-Mahdi's faction of the Umma Party, the Sudan African National Union (SANU), and the Islamic Charter Front (ICF). It was committed to passing a new constitution, to working toward peace in the south, to addressing regional issues, and to holding elections under parliament supervision by March 1968. But there was strong opposition. Southerners and Muslim leaders from Darfur, the Nuba Mountains, and the Red Sea Hills opposed the constitution and the government. These leaders wanted Islamists and southerners to work toward common goals and get to know each other better.

Unfortunately, each segment of the NFC was working toward achieving its own goals. Al-Mahdi wanted to be seen as a symbol of modernization and the heir of the ancient regime. SANU was more interested in regional independence and peace in the south, thus voted against Islamic provisions to the constitution. The goal of the ICF was to see the constitution passed because it was the key to its drive toward a complete Islamic state in Sudan. During an attempt at developing a new constitution, 40 Christian delegates boycotted the second reading in parliament in January 1968 in protest to its "dominant Islamic spirit."

The constitution continued to be debated, with the south calling for less Islamic wording and more clauses related to Christian causes and the north refusing to remove references to Sharia law. Al-Mahdi supported the Islamic constitution, and a final agreement was reached where an Islamic constitution was to be passed with the stipulation that points of disagreements would be put to a referendum (to put a public measure to a popular vote).

MILITARY RULE UNDER COLONEL JAFAR NIMEIRI (1969–1985)

Just two days after the Constituent Assembly adopted the constitution, Colonel Jafar Nimeiri and the army assumed power in a bloodless coup. The country was now ruled by the military Revolutionary Command Council. Nimeiri sought to apply a socialist approach to government and dissolved all traditional political parties. He suspended the existing constitution and took steps to reduce and eventually eliminate the economic power of the religious sects.

Now in full control, Nimeiri established a single-state party. This made it possible for him to nationalize the basic sectors of the economy, thereby making them government owned and controlled. He also began to formulate strategies for social development. Nimeiri called this the Sudanese Socialist Union. The Sudanese began to acquire weapons from their new ally, the Soviet Union. This cozy relationship would not last long. Nimeiri began to dissolve links with the Soviets when he was almost overthrown by a communist-led coup. With the civil war still raging, Nimeiri decided that political negotiations would be the only way to resolve conflicts.

In 1972, both the Sudanese government and the rebel forces of the south, known as the Southern Sudan Liberation Movement (SSLM), met in Addis Ababa, Ethiopia, for negotiations. The SSLM wanted complete autonomy, with a single federal government between the two. They argued that without a federal system, the central government would in practice be a northern government, not a national one. The negotiations proceeded to define what powers the central and regional government should have. In the end, the south was granted a large measure of autonomy. The southerners were given the right to have their own elected assembly and executive body. In addition, they were given recognition that their beliefs, languages, and traditions were equal in importance to those of the north.

The first round of fighting came to an end with the establishment of a regional government for the south. The agreement was ratified as the Regional Self-Government Act in March 1972 and was incorporated into Sudan's first permanent constitution in 1973. Following this agreement, Sudan received substantial amounts of aid and investment. Yet, the Southern Regional Government received on average only about 23 percent of the central government's grant for the special development budget throughout the 11 years of regional government.

In 1979, the U.S. oil company Chevron discovered petroleum deposits in the Bentiu District of the Upper Nile. When this occurred, Nimeiri attempted to deny the south's

The civil wars in Sudan have been the longest and deadliest wars of the twentieth century (1955–1972; 1983–2005). Although the second civil war officially ended in 2005, violent struggles continue in Darfur between the Sudanese military and Janjaweed (a northern Afro-Arab Sudanese militia group) on one side and the Sudan Liberation Army (SLA) and Justice and Equality Movement (JEM) on the other. Above, JEM fighters drive their armored vehicle to the Sudan-Chad border in northwest Darfur.

ownership of the oil. He redrew the boundaries between the north and south so that the reserves fell within the territorial control of the north. The south was convinced that the central government intended to plunder the newly discovered reserves for the benefit of the north, with the south standing to gain very little.

Nimeiri stirred up several other issues involving the use of and control over the Upper Nile water. He took land belonging to the indigenous farming and herding population and used it for the expansion of mechanized commercial farming. He also abolished the legally elected regional government and assembly in Juba and subdivided the south into three regions (each with a Nimeiri-appointed governor). Finally, in September 1983, Nimeiri imposed Sharia law on the whole population of Sudan, a move called the September Laws. This was the last straw for the southern Sudanese. In 1983, the region once again plunged into a long and bitter civil war between north and south.

By 1982, Sudan had received more U.S. aid than any other country in sub-Saharan Africa—$160 million in annual economic assistance and $100 million in military aid. However, when Nimeiri denounced Israel in 1983, the United States cut off this aid, creating massive economic difficulties. Meanwhile, refugees were flooding in from Ethiopia, which was undergoing severe drought and famine, placing further strain on Sudan's dwindling resources. Drought and famine were also plaguing much of the northern half of Sudan, including Darfur (north and south), Kordofan, and the Red Sea Hills. Faced with these problems, Nimeiri's power finally crumbled. Parliamentary elections held in 1986 declared the Umma Party as the new leading government with, once again, Sadiq Al-Mahdi as the leader.

SADIQ AL-MAHDI AND HASSAN AL-TURABI (1986–1989)

Following his election, al-Mahdi met with John Garang, the leader of the Sudan People's Liberation Movement (SPLM), whose armed wing was called the Sudan People's Liberation Army (SPLA). Garang and al-Mahdi discussed a peace plan in which al-Mahdi claimed he would repeal the September Laws. Under pressure, however, al-Mahdi suddenly backed down from the proposed arrangement.

His brother-in-law Hassan al-Turabi, who was a big influence on al-Mahdi, had a different idea. As leader of the newly organized National Islamic Front (NIF), he committed himself to the establishment of an Islamic state and was determined to enforce his interpretation of Islamic law, which included a penal code. He also opposed any sort of negotiations with the south.

GENERAL OMAR HASSAN AHMAD AL-BASHIR

In 1980, when Sadiq al-Mahdi seemed to be ready to begin negotiations with the south, he was ousted in a military coup led by General Omar Hassan Ahmad al-Bashir. General al-Bashir suspended the 1986 constitution and pushed for negotiations with the SPLM. Al-Bashir met with many criticisms from the West and other groups who were concerned about the displaced Sudanese people.

The new government also faced accusations of supporting terrorism. In fact, Osama bin Laden, the leader of al Qaeda, had moved to Sudan in 1991. During this period, al Qaeda established connections with other terrorist organizations with the help of its Sudanese hosts and Iran. While in Sudan, al Qaeda was involved in several terrorist attacks and guerrilla actions including the bombings of the U.S. embassies in Nairobi, Kenya, and Dar es Salaam, Tanzania. Sudan was implicated in the June 1995 assassination attempt on Egyptian president Hosni Mubarak. Its support for terrorists and increasing international isolation led to a U.S. cruise-missile attack on a Sudanese pharmaceutical factory in 1998. The U.S. claimed that the Sudanese factory was financed by bin Laden and was manufacturing chemical weapons. Sudan's government denied all accusations. In response to U.S., Egyptian, and Saudi pressures, bin Laden left Sudan in 1996.

The civil war began to spread northward. In November 1996, the National Democratic Alliance, the Democratic Unionist Party, the Umma Party, the Sudan Federation Forces, and the Legitimate Command of the Sudanese Army joined with the SPLM. They joined together mainly to battle the oppressive forces of the National Islamic Front (NIF), which was violating the political and civil rights of the south. President al-Bashir dismissed Hassan al-Turabi after a falling out. Al-Turabi had ambitions for an Islamic revolution throughout Africa and the Middle East, while al-Bashir held to the traditional view of Sudan as the home of the Arab elite.

On March 4, 2009, the International Criminal Court (ICC) charged Sudanese president Omar Hassan al-Bashir with five counts of crimes against humanity and war crimes. It was the first time the court indicted a sitting head of state. Al-Bashir has rejected the charges, and the prosecution is unlikely to be carried out.

After the terrorist attacks of September 11, 2001, U.S. president George W. Bush declared to the world, "Either you are with us, or you are terrorists." With this warning, al-Bashir began to attempt to improve relations with the United States. By July 20, 2002, negotiations between the south and the north resulted in the signing of the Machakos Protocol. The protocol reaffirms the priority status of unity, but grants the south the right of self-determination after a six-year period. By October 2002, the government and the SPLA (the armed wing of the SPLM) agreed to a ceasefire while negotiations continued.

The southern rebels and the government in Khartoum seemed to patch things up in January 2005 with a detailed peace agreement that ensured a permanent ceasefire and sharing of wealth and power. John Garang became the first vice president of the south. President al-Bashir formed a government of national unity as part of the deal. The SPLM later suspended its participation in the government, claiming that Khartoum was not honoring the 2005 peace deal. They later resumed participation in December 2007.

WILL AL-BASHIR BE ARRESTED?

The International Criminal Court (ICC) has charged President Omar al-Bashir with war crimes and crimes against humanity, and has issued an international warrant for his arrest. After months of deliberation, the judges convicted al-Bashir for playing an essential role in the murder, rape, torture, pillage, and displacement of large numbers of civilians in Darfur. The immediate reaction was huge pro al-Bashir rallies in Khartoum. President al-Bashir also expelled 13 humanitarian aid groups, such as Oxfam and Doctors without Borders, from Darfur. The departure of these agencies will create even more hardship, since in some places they provide the only medical services.

Only time will tell if al-Bashir will be arrested. In theory, he is subject to arrest if he ventures outside his country. In reality, that likely won't happen, particularly if he is careful in picking his countries and airports in which to land. Although many African leaders don't like what is happening in Sudan, the African Union and many African governments feel a kinship with al-Bashir. He therefore knows he is safe from the long reach of the Belgium-based ICC. So confident is he, in fact, that after the warrant was issued, while presiding at a dam dedication, he said the ICC should take the arrest warrant, "dissolve it in water, and drink it." Meanwhile the bleeding and suffering continue in Darfur, and Sudan remains a country divided and in turmoil.

In April 2010, Sudan conducted an election for president and the National Assembly. For the Sudanese, this election was very important. It marked the end of the five-year transitional period following the end of the most current bitter civil war. Many people, particularly those in the south, hoped that it would bring a change of government. However, President Omar al-Bashir and his party, the National Congress, won the election receiving early 70 percent of the votes. According to many observers, fraud was widespread. Politically, things seem to change very little in Sudan.

5

The Darfur Crisis

In 2004, Darfur, in western Sudan, became a central focus of international attention and outrage. The people of Darfur suffered incredible atrocities committed by the Sudanese government and its supporters. There were widespread killings, torture, rape, and imprisonment. The horrible mayhem also included widespread looting, forced displacement, the burning of homes and villages, and the theft and deliberate destruction of crops and cattle. It became a humanitarian crisis of unimaginable dimensions. The United Nations estimates that the five-year conflict left 300,000 people dead and 2.7 million more displaced. Although it is unusual to have a separate chapter devoted to a specific conflict, the atrocities and human suffering in Darfur warrant such attention.

The humanitarian toll was made worse by the remoteness of the area, restrictions by the Sudanese government on humanitarian operations, and conditions on the ground. Attacks by armed assailants on aid workers drastically reduced operations, and completely eliminated access to some areas of Darfur. In many areas, roads were under the control of roaming militias or armed opposition groups and numerous checkpoints were established for extorting money. Humanitarian aid convoys were regularly hijacked for the supplies they carried as well as for the vehicles themselves, and the drivers were assaulted, kidnapped, or murdered.

Despite international outrage and demands around the globe to end the brutality, the deadly conflict continued. Civilians became victims of shocking human rights violations and brutality.

THE ROOTS OF THE DARFUR CRISIS

Culturally, Darfur is an extremely complex place. Some 50 to 80 different ethnic and tribal groups create a complex mosaic of peoples unparalleled almost anywhere else in the world. Such diversity can lead to conflict, as it has in this troubled region. At the most basic level, two groups make up Darfur's population: Africans and Arabs. Africans, most of whom are settled farmers, were the original inhabitants of the region. Arabs, mainly nomadic camel and cattle herders, began pushing into the area in the fourteenth century. The Africans were rapidly converted to Islam, and today nearly all Darfurians are Muslims. For centuries, the two groups lived in relative peace. Anywhere in the world where settled farmers and nomadic herders live side-by-side, however, disputes arise. Most such conflicts arose over the often-contentious competition for resources between fixed farming communities and pastoral nomads. Such disputes were resolved through negotiations involving local leaders. In times past, people of Darfur were identified by race (physical appearance), or culture (including language and means of subsistence). Today, most Darfurians claim mixed ancestry as a result of centuries of intermarriage.

مركز حماية حقوق الطفولة والأمومة ـ ولاية شمال دارفور

This piece of art shows the devastation and horrors of the atrocities in Darfur. The Janjaweed attacked and burned villages; men, women, and children were shot; women and girls were raped; and Sudanese forces dropped bombs on the people and their homes.

Darfur's recorded history begins in the fourteenth century. For several centuries, Darfur existed as a self-governing state. By the mid-seventeenth century, Darfur's geographical location made it a thriving commercial hub. Situated between Mediterranean Europe and sub-Saharan Africa, slaves, ivory, ostrich feathers and other items moved northward to the Mediterranean as trade goods. Slaves were captured in raids against its neighbors and in wars of conquest within the surrounding region. In January 1917, Darfur became part of Sudan, which in turn was absorbed into the British Empire. The British, however, had little interest in Darfur. As a result it became a somewhat remote economic and political backwater and a pawn in power games.

It was not long before Darfur became embroiled in the conflicts raging around it. Many of the soldiers who fought for the government against the south were Darfurian recruits. Libya's controversial leader, Colonel Moammar al-Gadhafi (Qaddafi), used Darfur as a military base for his wars in Chad. His objective was to promote Arab supremacist tendencies. The attempt had devasting results, inflaming ethnic tensions, flooding the region with weaponry, and sparking the Arab-Fur War (1987–1989), in which thousands were killed and hundreds of Fur villages were burned. (*Darfur* means "Land of the Fur," the indigenous peoples of the region.) The people's suffering was made worse by a devastating famine in the mid-1980s, and the Sudanese government ignored Darfur and the plight of its suffering people.

When General Omar al-Bashir seized power in Sudan in 1989 he banned opposition parties, halted efforts toward peace to the region, and proclaimed *jihad* (holy war) against the non-Muslim south, regularly using Muslim Arab militias to do the fighting. Although al-Bashir depended on Muslim Darfur for political support, the program of "Arabization" further marginalized Darfur's African population.

WHO ARE THE JANJAWEED?

Janjaweed are fighters who often turn to violence in support of their fervent belief in Arab supremacy. The word *janjaweed* means "hordes" or "ruffians," but also sounds like "devil on horseback" in Arabic. Each of these meanings describes the group well. Most members are recruits from nomadic Arabic tribes, angry former soldiers, or criminal elements. They first appeared as a military force during the Arab-Fur War in the late 1980s. The Sudanese government recognized that the Janjaweed could be a powerful force in helping advance its vicious political agenda. It armed and trained the fighters and then turned them loose on the people of Darfur for a period of three years, from 1996 to 1998. In so doing, the Sudanese government used a military strategy in which it used ethnic militias to do its dirty work. Using Janjaweed fighters, the government could save money and also deny any role in the conflicts.

Pictured are the remains of a village in Tiero, in eastern Chad, after it was attacked by the Janjaweed and their Chadian allies. The Sudanese Arab horsemen called the Janjaweed and the Chadian rebel forces are working together to oust the governments in N'Djamena, the capital of Chad, and Darfur in Sudan.

Darfur was ripe for rebellion. The region was ravaged by drought and ethnic conflicts. It was an area in which grinding poverty and decades of political and cultural marginalization had taken a heavy toll on the people. In response to growing frustrations, two main rebel groups formed—the Sudan Liberation Army (SLA) and the Justice and Equality Movement (JEM). Both were responsible for a sharp increase in the number and ferocity of rebel attacks against government targets. By early 2003 the SLA and JEM had joined forces. Fighting as an alliance, they were able to inflict considerable damage on the increasingly ineffective Sudanese army.

By 2003, the government was losing control of the country. Faced with this bleak prospect, leaders decided to launch a counter attack against the combined forces of the SLA and JEM. The government fell back on an age-old source of conflict—competition over increasingly scarce land and water resources—to fuel the flames of dissention. Using this "excuse," the government gained support of the Janjaweed, who immediately began to attack settlements the government claimed had links to the rebels.

Critics blame the crisis in Darfur on the Sudanese government. The United States has labeled the crisis as genocide (an attempt to destroy an entire people). Refugees from Darfur say that following air raids by government aircraft, the Janjaweed would ride into the villages on horses and camels, slaughtering men, raping women, and stealing whatever they could find. The Sudanese government denies being in control of the Janjaweed. Sudan and Chad accuse each other of supporting their rebel groups. This has further increased the difficulty of the situation in Darfur.

Despite international outrage and demands to end the brutality, the deadly conflict continues. Darfur remains one of the world's worst humanitarian catastrophes. Civilians have become victims of horrendous human rights violations at the hands of the Sudanese government and the Janjaweed. As mentioned previously, the atrocities committed by these two aggressors have been monumental. One can only wonder when people's inhumanity to other people will end, and when the killings, torture, rape, looting, and other human rights abuses will end in Darfur.

WHAT CAUSED THE DARFUR CRISIS?

Many people blame competition for natural resources as the primary trigger of conflict in Darfur. Some blame global warming for triggering environmental problems that make natural resources even scarcer. In reality, the factors driving Darfur's conflict are much more complex.

In its 50 years of independence, Sudan has been plagued by constant conflicts. They are rooted in economic, political, social, and military domination by the small, powerful, and elite group of northern Sudanese that has been governing the country. Fighting in Darfur has continued off and on for at least 30 years. Until 2003, fighting was confined mainly to a series of local and tribal conflicts. Then these hostilities escalated into a full-scale military confrontation in all three Darfurian states. The conflict also frequently spills over into neighboring Chad and the Central African Republic.

The great drought and famine of 1984 and 1985 led to localized conflicts between herders and farmers in a struggle for diminishing resources. These hostilities led to the Arab-Fur War of 1987 to 1989.

The tragedy that began in 2003 was caused mainly by the government's response to rebellion. There were, however, many other causes of the conflict. They include historical grievances, local perceptions of race, demands for a fair sharing of power between different groups, and the inequitable distribution of economic resources and benefits. Other issues involve disputes over access to and control over increasingly scarce natural resources (land and water) and the spreading of arms and the militarization of young people. Finally, there was a total absence of democratic processes and numerous other issues related to governance. Local issues have been drawn into the wider political situation of Sudan.

Competition between herders and farmers is key to under-standing so many conflicts in East Africa, including the crisis in Darfur. Violence between tribes and ethnic groups are the most visible dividing lines, but the stories of these conflicts cannot be told without including underlying stresses on the environment and the population.

THE CLIMATE CHANGE FACTOR

Sudan, along with other countries in the Sahel belt, has suffered several long and devastating droughts during recent decades. The most severe drought occurred between 1980 and 1984, and was accompanied by widespread displacement and famine. The scale of historical climate change, as recorded in northern Darfur, is extraordinary: The drought has turned millions of acres (hectares) of already marginal semidesert grazing land into desert. Desertification has added significantly to the stress on the livelihoods of herding societies, forcing them to move south into wetter lands in order to find pasture.

The United Nations Environmental Program (UNEP) has identified categories of natural resources supposedly linked to the conflicts in Sudan. The list includes oil and gas reserves, Nile water, hardwood timber, rangeland and rain-fed agricultural land, and the associated water points. But in Sudan, use of land and economic resources are so complex that any summary of the issue is little more than a watered-down simplification. Traditional herding and farming societies in Sudan are not always clearly separated. In many areas, families, clans, and even entire tribes grow crops and raise animals.

Three groups may be identified in rural Sudan. First, there are the mainly farming societies/tribes; second, there are the nomadic livestock-rearing society/tribes; finally, are the owners and workers involved in mechanized agricultural schemes. The latter group includes business or government programs that support the development, mechanization, storage, transport, insurance, marketing, and use of new technologies to increase agriculture in a country. Directly or indirectly, these three groups depend on rainfall for their livelihood. While most of the recorded local conflicts take place within and between the first two groups, the mechanized farming group has triggered fighting by uncontrolled land grabs from the other two groups. For example, in the Nuba Mountains and in Blue Nile State, combatants reported that the expansion of mechanized agricultural schemes onto their land sparked the fighting, which then escalated and became part of the major north-south political conflict.

Throughout Sudan's recorded history, herders resisting the shrinkage and destruction of rangelands have been at the center of local conflicts. They compete with other groups for choice grazing land, move and graze livestock on cropland without consent from farmers, and force other herders and farmers off previously shared land.

MIGRATION AND ENVIRONMENTAL DESTRUCTION

In addition to untold human suffering, the conflict has taken a toll on the environment. Fighting often involved a "scorched earth" campaign in which fire was used as a weapon. This tactic was carried out by militias over large areas and resulted in huge numbers of civilian deaths, widespread destruction of villages and forests, and the displacement of huge numbers of victims fleeing to refugee camps for protection, food, and water.

The sheer number of displaced people in a refugee camp further degrades the environment. Extensive deforestation results from harvesting fuel wood for cooking, as well as from making bricks for housing. Today some camps in Darfur have run out of fuel wood supplies within walking distance, resulting in major fuel shortages.

SUDAN'S FORGOTTEN SLAVES

(The following tragic story of slavery in Sudan is based upon a BBC News report by Joseph Winter.) Nineteen years ago, Akech Arol Deng's wife and son were seized from their home in southern Sudan by an Arab militia. He has not seen them since. Deng believes that they are still alive and enslaved in northern Sudan. In 2007, the United Nations believed that 8,000 people (and as many as 200,000 according to some estimates) were working as slaves in the country. Although slavery has been banned worldwide for more than a century, according to the U.N. the horrendous practice is quite widespread in portions of

The Dinka is the single largest tribal group in southern Sudan, numbering about 2.5 to 3 million and 25 different sections. Some Dinka mark or scarify their face to celebrate graduation into adulthood. Within other groups, some female Dinka mark their face to signify a particular status. Today, many of the Dinka who had been abducted or given away by their parents are moving back south.

Africa, including Sudan. And sadly, no one appears to be doing anything to free today's slaves.

Sudan's government does not accept claims of slavery. It does admit that during the war thousands of people were abducted, but attributes the practice to an ancient tradition of hostage-taking by rival ethnic groups. A senior Sudanese government official, while denying that slavery exists in the country, acknowledged that the situation "[is] the same as when people were taken from West Africa to America."

In 1999, an internationally supported program was established to free abductees. Several thousand were found and returned home. By 2005, however, the program ran out of money, because for various reasons many donors pulled out.

Finding the parents and homes of children abducted up to 20 years ago is difficult and in many cases impossible. Many children, forced to adopt Islamic names, have forgotten their real names. Often they have no idea where they came from, or who their parents are. Some can be identified by facial scars from marks cut into their faces when young (a tradition among some tribes). Many youngsters simply end up with foster parents. Slavery is just one of many tragic outcomes of Sudan's long history of conflict.

6

Sudan's Economy

Very surprisingly, considering its past and present conditions, Sudan has one of the fastest growing economies in the world. The economic boom began when the first barrels of oil were exported to Singapore in 1999 and growth has continued since then. Between 2006 and 2007, the economy grew more than 10 percent. This was fueled mainly by oil exports and huge investments by Asian countries such as China and Singapore. Nevertheless, poverty is widespread. A recent estimate suggests that about 40 percent of the population lives below the poverty line. About 80 percent the population depends on subsistence agriculture, which has been severely affected by recent droughts and conflicts.

One way to measure the severity of economic deprivation is the Human Poverty Index (HPI-1). The HPI-1 measures a country's health conditions by the proportion of people who are not expected to survive past age 40. Sudan's HPI-1 as of 2004 was 34.4 percent. Another measure is the Human Development Index (HDI), developed by the United Nations. It compares life expectancy, literacy, education, and standard of living for 182 countries worldwide. In 2009, Sudan ranked 150, lower than any country in the Americas including struggling Haiti. So, you can see that while Sudan's economy prospers, the Sudanese government seems to care very little about the Sudanese people, particularly those in the south. In this chapter you will learn about Sudan's past and present economic conditions.

SUDAN'S ECONOMY THROUGH TIME

Sudan has not always been dirt poor. In fact, over the past several thousand years there have been times when at least some of its people prospered. The Nile River has long been an artery of trade between present-day Sudan and Egypt. Khartoum is located at the confluence (juncture) of the White and Blue Nile rivers, both of which served as links to lands and riches lying to the south. From very early times, Sudan was actively involved in trade focusing upon the Nile and Red Sea. Looking westward, it was also in an ideal position to trade with empires located along the southern margin of the Sahara Desert. The Nubian empires, including Kush and later Meroe, grew and prospered because of these trade links. Gold, ivory, and incense were major trade items that moved northward to Egypt. So were slaves who served as servants, concubines, and soldiers in Egypt. Grain was a major trade item from Egypt.

Meroe expanded linkages with the Red Sea coast, where it carried on a lively exchange with traders from Arab lands and as far eastward as India. There is evidence, although it remains hotly disputed among archaeologists and historians, that iron metallurgy began in Meroe. Ancient ironworks have been discovered there, and it is believed that iron smelting techniques may have diffused from Meroe westward across the Sahel and savanna lands to West Africa.

CULTURE AND ECONOMIC CHANGE

When judging Sudan's economy, one must keep in mind that a commercial economy—one measured by dollars (or local currency), rather than survival—is recent. This is particularly true in Africa where many people, even today, are pretty much self-sufficient and live outside the cash economy. Their labor and its results are not measured monetarily. Hence, they do not appear in a nation's gross domestic product or any other measure of wealth. This is extremely misleading. Many people who depend upon their own labor, such as farming and herding, are able to provide for themselves quite well. Such rural families may, indeed, be much better off in terms of providing for themselves than are many of their counterparts who live in a city and earn wages.

For millennia, such people survived and most lived quite well in the land that is now Sudan. Three things have happened to minimize their living standards: cultural change, almost constant conflict, and political chaos. During recent centuries and certainly since the dawn of the Industrial Revolution, culture has changed. Self-reliant traditional folk cultures were left in the economic wake of urban, industrial, commercial peoples. And as is described above, with these cultural adjustments also came a change in the way economic (providing the things one needs to survive) success is measured. Simply stated, in times past, all peoples practiced a subsistence economy; some remained traditional, whereas others moved ahead.

A second problem, and one that has been incredibly disruptive to the lives of so many Sudanese, is the seemingly endless conflict. It is difficult if not impossible for a country's economy to grow or its citizens to prosper when their land is torn by strife. Would you want to go into a field to work on crops or watch over your livestock knowing that at any moment you could be kidnapped or even killed?

Finally, good government and economic growth go hand-in-hand. When a government is effective and a country is politically stable, people are willing to invest in its development. Neither citizens nor foreigners, on the other hand, are willing to invest their financial resources in a corrupt and poorly governed country.

There are, of course, many other reasons for Sudan's relatively poor economy. Many nomads have moved into urban areas. They swell the need for services, yet lack the education and skills needed to compete successfully in an urban economy. The civil war has been extremely disruptive, because it has slowed or even closed down many economic activities. Basically, as has been stressed time and time again in this book, Sudan has suffered because of ineffective government and seemingly constant civil conflict.

OVERVIEW OF THE ECONOMY

In 2009, Sudan's per capita gross domestic product—purchasing power parity (GDP-PPP) was $2,300. (Purchasing power parity is the amount of goods and services that could be purchased with U.S. dollars.) The country ranks 181 among the some 220 countries for which data are available. Although its standing is quite low, Sudan ranks in the top 25 percent of African states in this category.

Figures such as GDP-PPP can be extremely misleading, particularly when they are applied to a poor country such as Sudan. Forty percent of Sudanese, for example, live below the country's poverty line. About 19 percent of the people are unemployed, but this only tells part of the country's story of poverty. When underemployment is added, nearly half of all Sudanese lack adequate employment and incomes. This category includes people who have jobs, but are unable to make a decent living.

In Sudan, the economy is experiencing rapid change. Such improvements surely will accelerate if peace comes to this wartorn land and its government becomes more responsible to its people. Let's take a brief look at each of the three major sectors of the economy: primary, secondary, and tertiary.

Primary Industries

Primary industries are those based upon the extraction or use of natural resources. They include agriculture (both farming and herding), mining, logging, and fishing. Generally speaking, the more developed a country is economically, the less it will depend upon primary economic activities. In the United States, for example, less than 1 percent of the population is engaged in any of the primary industries, and only 1.2 percent of the GDP is produced by them. In Sudan, 80 percent of the labor force is engaged in agriculture (data are not available for other activities within the primary sector). Yet farming and herding contribute only about one-third of the country's GDP. This suggests that most agriculture is for subsistence, rather than commercial production. For the most part, it is primitive and relatively unproductive. People raise crops or herd livestock for their own consumption, rather than for the market. This reliance upon subsistence farming ensures that a large percentage of the country's population will remain at or below the poverty line for years to come.

In the past, agriculture has been the backbone of Sudan's economy, traditionally accounting for more than 90 percent of the country's exports. During recent decades, several factors have contributed to a decline in Sudan's agricultural productivity. They include a lack of investment in agricultural technologies and development, civil conflicts, droughts, and a sharp drop in rural population.

Most of Sudan's commercial agricultural production occurs along the Nile River and its upper tributaries, particularly in the area of Khartoum, and in the east-central region. Many crops are grown for the domestic market. Grain crops include millet, wheat, and sorghum. Cassava (sweet manioc, or tapioca), sweet potatoes, and groundnuts (peanuts) also

Agriculture remains Sudan's most important sector. The crops are susceptible to drought, however, due to reliance on unreliable rainfall.

are basic staples of the Sudanese diet and are grown primarily for local consumption. So are mangos, papayas, and bananas. Cotton is Sudan's major crop, although its production has decreased during recent years. Other commercial crops grown for export include sugarcane (for sugar), gum arabic, sesame, and peanuts.

Nomadic herding has long been a traditional economic activity throughout much of northern Africa, including Sudan. Today, however, livestock-related activities are in sharp decline throughout the country. The severe droughts and widespread conflicts of recent decades have taken their toll on herders and herding. Some previously nomadic people have begun to farm. Most former nomads, however, have moved to Khartoum or some other urban area. This change has been so rapid that Sudan is one of the world's fastest urbanizing countries.

Some commercial logging occurs in the south, but it is not a major contributor to the country's economy. The same can be said for the limited commercial fishing activity in the Nile River and Red Sea. Neither activity is of more than local importance. Mining and oil extraction are also primary industries. Sudan has small amounts of copper, gold, and other minerals, but their economic importance is negligible. Recent development of rich petroleum deposits, however, has created a huge economic boom in Sudan. What it means to the country is discussed later in this chapter.

Secondary Industries

Secondary industries include processing, manufacturing, and construction. Basically, they involve taking primary products and turning them into useful items. This activity involves about 29 percent of the Sudanese workforce, but contributes only 7 percent of the country's GDP. Again, we find that Sudanese industry is very ineffective.

Most industrial development is based upon the processing of agricultural products. Cotton ginning and textile industries, for example, process domestic cotton for export. Sugar and edible oils also are processed from sugarcane and sesame seeds. Recently, the country has begun manufacturing small automobiles, trucks, and heavy military equipment at plants in Khartoum. A cement industry supports Sudan's thriving construction boom. And Sudan's oil boom has spurred the development of refineries in Khartoum and Port Sudan. Pharmaceuticals also are manufactured and exported.

Within the secondary sector of the economy, the construction industry is experiencing huge growth. During recent years Sudan has benefitted greatly from direct foreign economic investment. More than $3.5 billion was invested in 2006 (the most recent year for which figures are available at the time of writing). Construction of desperately needed new highways and bridges is booming. Khartoum is experiencing a huge

Hundreds of Sudanese hold banners praising President al-Bashir to celebrate the opening of a hydroelectric dam on the Nile River at Meroe in northern Sudan on March 3, 2009. The hydropower project, the largest to be built along the Nile in 40 years and the largest international project that Chinese contractors have ever participated in, will increase power generating capacity from about 30 percent to 90 percent. Still, this project has displaced about 6,000 farmers.

building boom. Plans are underway to build a new oil refinery at Port Sudan. But during the first decade of the twenty-first century, no project has been more ambitious or costly than Sudan's new Meroe Dam.

With the help of about $1.8 billion, mostly from China, Sudan has constructed the huge Merowe Dam on the Nile River about 220 miles (350 km) north of Khartoum. The multi-purpose dam is 5.6 miles (9 km) wide and has the capacity to generate 1,250 megawatts of much-needed hydroelectric energy. When filled, the reservoir will extend upstream (south-ward) for nearly 110 miles (177 km) and hold about 20 percent of the Nile's annual flow. It will improve the domestic water supply for millions of people and also supply water to irrigate crops. When President al-Bashir inaugurated the dam upon its completion in 2009, he declared it a project of the century and a pride of Sudan, the Arabs, and the world.

Tertiary Industries

Tertiary industries are those that contribute services of any kind. They include financial institutions, health care, police and fire protection, and education. Sales are included, as are transportation and communication, secretarial assistance, various media, restaurants, and various businesses that serve the tourist industry. Throughout the economically developed world, about 75 percent of the workforce is engaged in the service sector. And a comparable percentage of a country's GDP also is produced by tertiary activities. In the United States, for example, roughly 77 percent of both the workforce and GDP involve the provision of various services. For Sudan, the data are more than a decade old, but it is probable that only about 15 percent of the workforce is engaged in service-related industries. Because most people involved in the tertiary sector are urban and educated, they contribute disproportionately to a nation's economy. In Sudan, the estimated 15 percent of the workforce engaged in the tertiary sector contributes nearly 40 percent of the country's GDP. In the future, this proportion certainly will increase.

Most of Sudan's service industries are found in and around Khartoum. With a metropolitan area population approaching 9 million, the majority of which are literate, the region has a huge, able, and eager workforce.

SUDAN'S OIL BOOM

The search for oil began in Sudan more than a half century ago and became more intense during the mid-1970s. By the early 1980s, the long and costly search paid off when an American firm, Chevron, struck oil in Upper Nile Province in southern Sudan. A second find, the Abu Jabra oil field, was made later on the edge of South Darfur and Southern Kordofan. Production and export got underway in 2000. Its importance to the Sudanese economy is evident in the fact that by 2010, oil accounted for more than 80 percent of the country's export earnings. From the fields, oil is transported by pipelines to refineries in Khartoum and Port Sudan. Nearly all of the petroleum is exported to China, with some going to other East Asian countries. According to some estimates, production already has peaked. Revenues, however, will continue to fill the country's financial coffers for years to come. Some experts believe that, with the end of hostilities in the country, further explorations may discover new deposits within the country.

PROSPERITY IS UNEQUAL IN SUDAN

During recent years, many Sudanese have begun to prosper as they never have before. This is particularly true for those living in the northern part of the country. Sadly, however, most residents of the country's war-ravaged south and the Darfur region live in grinding poverty. The south remains underdeveloped and poor. For many southern Sudanese, there seems to be little hope for the future. They believe, and justifiably, that their country and its government have forgotten them. Worse yet, their government seems not to care at all about their plight.

Southern Sudan: Exploited and Poor

Historically, the south has been subservient to the people and the cities in northern Sudan. During the time of slave trading, non-Muslim people in the south frequently were captured and exported as slaves to the Arabs. In terms of access, even today nearly all transportation routes focus upon Khartoum and other northern cities. Yet the south possesses far and away the country's greatest wealth of natural resources, including its rich oil deposits. The north, however, continues to be the major focus of Sudan's development and economic growth.

This is the reason for the huge differences in economic development between northern and southern Sudan. The north (Khartoum/Omdurman) has always received the best care, especially due to its prime location near the Nile, as well as its closeness to Egypt. The south, on the other hand, has always been exploited. With the discovery of oil in southern Sudan's As Sudd region, this exploitation of resources favoring the north certainly has continued. Many southerners have actually suffered as a result of oil development. Thousands of villagers were forcefully evicted from their land to make way for oil field development. Many lost their homes and saw their traditional economic livelihoods jeopardized.

DEVELOPMENT CHALLENGES

Sudan imports foodstuffs, manufactured goods, refinery and transport equipment, medicines and chemicals, textiles, and wheat. The country needs to become more self-sufficient in the production of these commodities. It exports oil and petroleum products, cotton, sesame, livestock, groundnuts, gum arabic, and sugar. Textiles are another import to Sudan, even though the country's major crop is cotton, and ancient skills such as spinning and weaving are deeply rooted in the Sudanese heritage. For decades, cotton exports contributed about 20 percent of Sudan's foreign trade. Yet, although Sudanese cotton is recognized internationally for its high quality, the country is importing foreign textiles. Clearly more attention needs to be directed toward the agricultural sector.

Today, Sudan depends upon only a couple items as the mainstays of its export economy. This dependence can have very serious consequences. When prices rise, the country prospers, as it has with recent oil exports. But when prices drop sharply, the results can be catastrophic not only to the economy, but to government and society as well. Today, Sudan's export economy is almost totally reliant upon oil exports. When the oil runs out, what then will Sudan rely upon?

In conclusion, Sudan is a country with numerous economic possibilities. Sadly, throughout most of its history, it has fallen far short of reaching those potentials. Most of its people continue to be impoverished, in poor health, poorly educated, and limited in terms of meaningful life options. Greater prosperity will come if Sudan can achieve a lasting peace and if the country's government becomes responsible and responsive to the needs of it people.

7

Living in Sudan Today

I t is impossible to write a "Living in Sudan Today" chapter that applies to all groups of people in the country. Ways of living among different groups of Sudanese vary greatly. In Khartoum and other northern cities, life is pretty much like it is in cities everywhere. There are, of course, cultural differences such as language and religion, but urban life is fairly similar whether in Khartoum, Kobe, Kaliningrad, or Kansas City. For many Sudanese, particularly those living in the north, life is improving. But the differences between the "have" and "have not" elements of Sudan's population remain huge.

Were you to visit the capital city, Khartoum, you would see a bustling urban area that is "modern" in nearly all respects. You would notice people going about their business pretty much as they do in the United States, Canada, and elsewhere. Many construction projects attest to the country's current economic boom. There, hopes for a peaceful and more prosperous future rise along with the city's skyline. Elsewhere, in places such as Darfur and many of the more remote areas of the south, conditions are desperate. Grinding poverty, poor health and sanitation, illiteracy, and shattered dreams are commonplace.

To greatly simplify Sudan's tremendous cultural diversity, we must think in terms of dualisms. For example, there are nomadic desert people of the north and the sedentary savanna and woodland farming people of the south. The north is dominated by people of Nubian physical features, whereas those of the south are Negroid. Most northerners are of Arabic culture; they follow the Islamic faith and speak Arabic. In the south African culture dominates; native religions are most commonly followed, and Bantu languages are spoken. Of greatest importance, however, is the dualism of economic well-being that exists between the richer north and dirt poor south.

HEALTH ISSUES

Widespread poverty, civil conflicts, and government inaction have combined to make health care facilities nearly nonexistent in Sudan. This is particularly true in the south, where nearly all medical facilities were destroyed during the civil war. Eventually, a few were rebuilt by the Sudan Peoples' Liberation Movement (SPLM) and controlled by government forces in Malakal, Waw, and Juba. Following the war, rebuilding efforts were severely hindered by the lack of funds and inadequate medical supplies. Because of the conflict and widespread poverty, the private medical care sector also was in shambles. More recently, the situation in Darfur has added to the country's medical miseries. Malnutrition, war-related injuries, and disease are widespread. The most common illnesses continue to be malaria, dysentery, and tuberculosis. AIDS also is widespread, particularly in the south. It also presents a growing problem in Khartoum, because many refugees from the south have sought safety in the city.

Malaria

Although the incidence of malaria has decreased since 2000, the disease continues to be Sudan's number one killer. In 1998, the government began to strengthen malaria control and the effort has been quite effective. A national 10-year strategic plan was developed in 2001, which resulted in the Malaria Free Initiative in 2002. These and other initiatives are extremely important to the physical well being of the Sudanese people. Unfortunately, floods that hit Sudan in 2007 caused an increase in the mosquito population and an upsurge in malaria infections. In response, the government and participating health organizations distributed 1.6 million mosquito nets in affected areas of the country.

Tuberculosis

Tuberculosis (TB) is another major killer in Sudan. According to the World Health Organization (WHO), in 2007 there were 243 cases per 100,000 people reported in the country. In southern Sudan alone, an estimated 18,500 people get the disease and 5,300 do annually. Unlike malaria, which is insect-transmitted, tuberculosis is a contagious disease passed from individual to individual. It is caused by bacteria and is spread through the air when people who have the disease spit, cough, or sneeze. TB attacks the lungs, but can also affect the central nervous system, the lymphatic system, the joints and bones, and even the skin. In southern Sudan case detection is still very low, but once identified, treatment achieves an 80 percent success rate. Destruction of the health infrastructure due to war, the lack of equipment such as microscopes, and the lack of health personnel all have contributed to the epidemic.

Meningitis

Sudan is located within the "Meningitis Belt" that stretches from Senegal to Ethiopia. Meningitis is an inflammation of the membranes that cover the brain and the spinal cord. It is an infection caused by viruses or microorganisms. Outbreaks commonly occur during the dry season as dust storms blow around bacteria attached to dust particles. In 2007, southern Sudan reported 12,000 meningitis cases. Currently health organizations working in Sudan have stockpiled 500,000 vaccines in case an outbreak occurs.

THE HEALTH CARE SYSTEM

Although many efforts have been made to improve the health care system, there are few services whether in government or non-government controlled areas. The government-controlled health network is arranged into three tiers. The first tier provides primary healthcare units, dressing stations, dispensaries, and health centers that include labs and X-ray units, but no in-patient ward. The second level has two separate parts. One component is rural hospitals and the other consists of specialized and teaching hospitals that offer more developed services. About 95 percent of all facilities are of the primary level category, whereas the two higher levels make up only about 5 percent of the health care network.

THE PLIGHT OF WOMEN AND CHILDREN

An African proverb says: "When two elephants fight, it is the grass that suffers." For most practical purposes, women and children are the grass that suffers from Sudan's unending conflicts and wars. Typically, they are the ones who are most affected by hostilities. In Darfur, for example, the Janjaweed use rape as a weapon of war. Yet President Omar al-Bashir denies this, saying that rape is unknown to the people and culture of Sudan or Darfur. Therefore, it "does not exist," simply because the country's president denies its existence!

Women are commonly victims of sexual and gender-based violence, especially in conflict zones. Unfortunately for these victims, it is a cultural taboo to discuss rape. In fact, many victims are shamed by their families if they report being raped. It also has been reported that in Darfur, many women have mental health problems. A recent study revealed that many displaced women in south Darfur and western Sudan suffer from depression and experience suicidal thoughts. In addition, displaced women suffer from many health problems due to general neglect. They have high pregnancy rates, poor health services while they are pregnant, and high rates of childbirth with no skilled attendants. As a result, the region has an alarmingly high infant mortality rate.

A 2003 demographic health survey of Sudan revealed that nearly two-thirds of all girls between the ages of 9 and 13 in rural areas are married. Many young girls are forced to marry at an early age because their poor families need some sort of income. One tragic result of this practice is that in 2008, southern Sudan had the world's highest pregnancy-related death rate.

SHARIA AND SUDANESE LIFE

Sudan has been in the news recently because of Sharia enforcement issues. Here, two examples are cited that have gained international attention. They illustrate how strict the law is and why many people, particularly non-Muslims in Muslim dominated countries, oppose the imposition of Sharia.

Forbidden Slacks

In July 2009, Lubna al-Hussein and 12 other Sudanese women were arrested for wearing slacks in public. Ten of the women immediately pled guilty to the "crime," were given 10 lashes, and released. Al-Hussein requested a trial. As a journalist for the United Nations, she was in a position to publicize her case, which rapidly gained international attention. A judge found al-Hussein guilty of violating Sudan's decency laws. But faced with a mounting international public outcry, he imposed a fine the equivalent of about US$200, but spared up to 40

Sudanese journalist Lubna Ahmed al-Hussein (*center*) leaves the court after a final hearing in the "trousers case" on September 7, 2009. Al-Hussein had been arrested with 12 other women for wearing pants in a Khartoum restaurant in July. She was spared a whipping but was fined 500 Sudanese pounds ($200). The journalist commented that she would rather go to jail than pay the fine.

lashes that could have been administered in accordance with Islamic law.

Islamic law calls for women to dress modestly, but the law is vague. According to Article 152 of Sudan's penal code, anyone "who commits an indecent act which violates public morality *or wears indecent clothing*" [emphasis the author's] can be fined and lashed up to 40 times. The strict law was implemented in 1991 by President al-Bashir, two years after he took power in an Islamic fundamentalist-inspired coup.

At the hearing, dozens of men in traditional Muslim clothing confronted about 150 of Hussein's mostly female supporters. As the women chanted "No to whipping!" the men shouted that women in trousers were prostitutes and demanded harsh punishment for al-Hussein. Riot police intervened and about 40 women were arrested and later released. At least one woman was taken to the hospital after being beaten.

As you can imagine, al-Hussein's case has gained international attention from many groups, including those that promote women's right. What would you do if you were arrested for being female and wearing your favorite pair of jeans? Would you admit to "guilt" (in the existing system), and simply pay the fine, take your flogging, or go to jail? Or would you fight for what you believe to be your rights?

Wrong Name for a Teddy Bear

Recently, a British schoolteacher faced up to 40 lashes and six months in prison for allowing her students to name a class teddy bear "Muhammad." Authorities said that naming a stuffed animal Muhammad was an insult to Islam. It all began in September 2007 when Gillian Gibbons, who taught at one of Sudan's most exclusive private schools, began a project on animals.

As part of the project, she asked the class to name a teddy bear. Almost unanimously, the class decided upon "Muhammad," one of the most common names in the Muslim world and the name of Islam's holy prophet. As part of the exercise, Gibbons told her students to take the bear home, photograph it, and write a diary entry about it. The entries were collected in a book called "My Name Is Muhammad." Most of her students were Muslim children from wealthy Sudanese families. When some parents saw the book, however, they complained to the government, insisting that naming a toy animal "Muhammad" was an insult to the prophet. When convicted, thousands of Sudanese took to the streets of Khartoum demanding death to the teacher who, they believed, had insulted Islam. But after being sentenced to 15 days in jail, however, she was pardoned by President al-Bashir.

THE LANDMINE PROBLEM

Sudan's never-ending wars have left a legacy of dangerous and often deadly landmines. The problem began as early as World War II. Most landmines in the north were laid when the British and Germans were fighting in the border area between Sudan and Libya and Egypt. Unfortunately, those mines were not removed and today, nearly seven decades later, they continue to kill nomadic people and livestock. Recent conflicts have only added to the landmine problem. In the south, mines have killed many people since the war ended in 2005. Officials claim that the government is committed to the extraction of landmines in the area. But it is unable to cover the entire area because of the cost and lack of funds. Sadly, because culture and traditions dictate that women work on farms, most landmine victims are female.

A 1997 landmine assessment by a branch of the U.N. found that landmines and explosives pose a threat in about one-third of Sudan. Southern Sudan alone had an estimated 500,000 to 2 million landmines. In fact, the government estimates that there are two landmines for each person in southern Sudan! By 2010, Sudan counted more than 700,000 amputees from mines and similar explosives.

Despite the removal of tens of thousands of the deadly devices, in 2009 it was estimated that some 2 million landmines remain. They pose a threat in an area of about 40,000 square miles (100,000 sq km). Four large areas of the country have huge landmine problems—the south, southwest, southeast, and northwest. Despite the ongoing efforts to de-mine, the problem remains very serious. The de-mining effort is poorly funded and faces many obstacles. Although large areas have been cleared, some areas such as Darfur are being replanted with the deadly devices. Additionally, wind and water move mines around, and records of which areas have been cleared are out of date and unreliable.

Farmers and shepherds throughout the country are primary targets of Sudan's landmines. Passable roads have been major targets for planting mines and continue to be in Darfur. Mines are also placed under fruit trees and by scarce water sources. Many times the mines are not even buried in the soil: They are placed among tufts of thick grass or wrapped in plastic bags and set in shallow pools or streams.

The threat of landmines makes life in Sudan unpredictable. Do you stay on the grass or on the road? Do you avoid the forests, the fields, or the streams? There are no right answers in Sudan. Consequently, the threat of disability or death from landmines has left rural populations, including farmers and herders, confused, frightened, and often inactive. Humans are not the only victims of Sudan's landmines. Animals also are affected by them. It is estimated that landmines kill an estimated 200 to 400 cows every day. As a result, livestock populations have declined. This is particularly troubling in a country where personal wealth and status is often determined by the size and well-being of one's livestock. Landmines have also affected the region's natural environment. Much of the wildlife, for example, has either been killed or has fled the region.

FEMALE DE-MINERS

Clearing the landmines is a difficult and very dangerous task performed only by very brave people. De-miners face serious injury or even death from their activities. One might think that only real "macho" men would work as de-miners. In Sudan, however, women do much of the de-mining. As you can imagine, the work is dangerous and extremely demanding. Most of it is done by teams, many of which are composed entirely of females. Team members work in shifts of perhaps 45 minutes to an hour in the scorching sun while wearing a heavy protective vest. While working, they wear thick face shields that make it impossible to drink water until their welcome break. They

In 2005, training for the first female de-mining team in Sudan began. They have had to struggle to convince others they can do the job, which is regarded by many as a role for a man. Clearing landmines, especially in one of the most dangerous regions in the nation, Mile 38, is hard work but the work of providing communities with land for agriculture and trade is worth the effort.

walk along the ground slowly, searching every inch of ground to ensure that it is safe.

QUALITY OF LIFE DETERMINED TODAY BY GEOGRAPHY

To summarize living in Sudan today, the quality of life very much depends upon where you live—your geography. If you live in the north, life may be fine. You worry about the effects of drought, but you live in relative peace and security. This is particularly true if you are a Muslim. If you live in the south, however, your life is unpredictable. Violence, limited transportation and communication facilities, limited public services, and grinding poverty all present challenges. If you live in one of Darfur's refugee camps, life is almost unbearable. There are severe food shortages, poor sanitation conditions, and the constant fear of violence and crime. In Sudan, geography—location, location, location—really does matter!

KHARTOUM AND OMDURMAN

The twin cities of Khartoum and Omdurman form Sudan's population, political, economic, and cultural core. Khartoum is the national capital, but Omdurman is the country's largest city, with an estimated population of 3 million. Originally established in 1884 as a military headquarters, Omdurman grew rapidly as an unplanned town of adobe (mud) houses. Today, it is a major commercial center. The Islamic University of Omdurman, founded in 1912, is widely known and respected.

Khartoum was founded in 1821 as an outpost for the Egyptian military. It became a major regional trading center and Sudan's capital when independence was gained in 1956. The estimated population of Khartoum in 2009 was about 2.2 million, with a total of around 8 million living in the immediate surrounding areas (which includes Omdurman).

Other important northern cities include Port Sudan, the country's chief seaport located on the Red Sea. The city is linked to Khartoum by both highway and railroad. Kassala, located east of Khartoum near the border with Eritrea, is an important agricultural area, with cotton being the major crop. It, too, is linked to Khartoum by both highway and rail linkages.

JUBA AND WAW

Juba is a city of about 250,000 and the regional capital of southern Sudan. Surprisingly, Juba is not linked to the north by either railroad or improved highway. Instead, it has much closer ties to neighboring Kenya, Uganda, and the Democratic Republic of the Congo. Today Juba is a commercial center for

Khartoum (which means "end of an elephants trunk" in Arabic) serves as the political, cultural, and economic capital of Sudan. It is located at the meeting point of the White Nile and the Blue Nile. The city has a thriving economy, with several projects taking place, including the construction of a new airport, five hotels, and the $4 billion Al-Mogran Development Project.

tobacco, coffee, and chilies. Its location on the Nile and road connections with outlying areas have helped it become a commercial center for the surrounding agricultural areas.

Other major cities of the south include Nimule, located on the border with Uganda and on the Nile, and Bor, located north of Juba along the Nile. Malakal is a city located in east-central Sudan in the As Sudd marsh. The west-central city of Nyala is a road and railway terminus and a safe haven for Darfur refugees.

WILL PEACE LAST?

The peace deal signed by the north and south in January 2005 brought a period of relative calm and stability to the region—

despite recent scattered violence. About 2 million displaced people have returned to south Sudan. They hope to rebuild their lives and play a part in creating a new country. Most residents of Akobo and elsewhere in the south do not want southern Sudan to remain joined to the north. Life continues to be hard in southern Sudan and development lags far behind that in the north. For example, south Sudan is the size of Texas or Canada's Alberta Province, yet it has only 12.5 miles (20 km) of hard-surface roads! Transportation is either by boat along the Nile and its tributaries, or along dirt roads that become impassible during the rainy season. The UN peacekeeping force there, one of the biggest in the world, travels by plane or helicopter.

For most Sudanese, particularly those in the south, life today continues to be difficult and uncertain. The situation in Darfur remains chaotic, with widespread human suffering. A vast cultural chasm continues to separate north and south. The gap includes government influence and services, economic opportunity, language, religious following, and human well-being.

CHAPTER

8

Sudan Looks Ahead

Today, life in Sudan is changing for most people, and many of the changes are for the best. Nomads are settling down, with many of them becoming farmers. Many rural people, including some former nomads, are moving to the cities. Only about 4 of 10 Sudanese live in urban places today, but the urban population is growing rapidly. The way of life experienced by city people is often much better than that of their rural counterparts. This is particularly true in extremely poor countries and lands torn apart by conflict.

Unfortunately, Sudan's government continues its longstanding tradition of being quite flawed, and 21 years of civil war and the current conflict in Darfur certainly have imposed a huge social and economic burden on the country and its people. The government still denies aiding the Janjaweed in its widespread atrocities, including rape and murder.

Nonetheless, new development programs have begun to encourage investments and generate revenue for the Sudanese people. Ever-increasing amounts of time and money are being poured into humanitarian efforts. Optimism is growing because Sudan has so many natural resources, including huge deposits of oil and natural gas. Throughout its history as a self-governing country, Sudan's government officials have endured many hardships to maintain the country as an Islamic state. Unfortunately, ever-increasing amounts of corruption have failed to bring Sudan into an Islamic state of being.

THE FUTURE OF SUDAN'S ECONOMY

There is no doubt that Sudan's economy has suffered many setbacks, resulting in the country being impoverished. Two decades of bitter civil war in the south, followed by the Darfur conflict, have taken a severe toll on economic activity. The country lacks an adequate transportation and communication infrastructure. This is true even in many urban areas. Much of the population continues to rely on subsistence agriculture and a largely self-sustaining barter economy. These issues and others ensure that much of Sudan's population will remain at or below the poverty line for years.

Nonetheless, Sudan's average per capita income is rising rapidly. Sudan began exporting crude oil in the last quarter of 1999, resulting in a huge boost to the country's gross domestic product. However, not everyone is enjoying the fruit of Sudan's newfound prosperity. Most of the benefits find their way to Khartoum and the 8 million people living in its metropolitan area.

POLITICS AND PEACE

Sudan's peace process has gained some momentum. Much of the progress is the result of the U.S. peace proposal begun in 2001 by John Danforth, former President George W. Bush's special envoy for peace in Sudan. Previous initiatives in 1992,

Modern Khartoum caters to the expatriate (foreign) communities and wealthy locals. New cafés, ice cream parlors, and restaurants are continually being opened as well as centers to get together, like sailing clubs and international clubs. Still, it is important to remember that northern Sudan is governed by Sharia law and is very strict.

1994, and 1998 sought to end the conflict, yet failed to achieve lasting peace for Sudan.

However, the recent U.S. involvement in the search for peace in Sudan has brought some hope. In addition to the U.S. efforts, the Swiss negotiated a ceasefire agreement for the conflict in the Nuba Mountain region. The British government has also become involved. There are also intensive diplomatic efforts and activities by other European countries, such as Norway. Several African countries also are involved in the effort to bring peace to Sudan. We can only hope that all these efforts will lead to a just and lasting end of hostilities.

Sudan is the largest country in Africa and a nation of tremendous diversity in terms of its culture, including religion, ethnicity, and languages. In order to accommodate these diverse elements, the aspirations and demands of many different peoples must be met. That, in itself, is a tall order. The responsibility falls to the Sudanese people to explore remedies for the underlying root causes of the conflict that has divided them for so long.

One such solution is a genuine constitution that will embrace all Sudanese regardless of their culture, including language, religion, social orientation, or ethnic origin. As a result of the widespread diversity, there is a need for a much more equal distribution of power. Different ethnic groups, for example, must be allowed to exercise a greater degree of self-governance. The governments that have ruled Sudan since independence have tried various forms of governance. They have ranged from military dictatorships to democratic regimes. Yet none of them have been successful.

The repeated failures can be attributed to the fact that power has always remained with the central government, despite promises of decentralization and federation. This may be due to the lack of political leaders who speak for the desires and aspirations of all people of Sudan, rather than their own self-interests. If unity is to be achieved for Sudan, there is a genuine need for a unitary constitution that will encourage a strong democratic political environment. More importantly, this unifying constitution needs to enshrine the ideals and aspirations of all the people. The Sudanese government needs to take steps to ensure that all of the regions obtain their share of power and an equal share of the economic development and wealth of the nation. This will be a huge catalyst for providing greater self-rule for Sudanese in all parts of the country.

Improving the quality of the educational system and ensuring universal access to education for all Sudanese children is vitally important. Fortunately, this is the focus of several ongoing projects. One such project, sponsored by the Department for International Development (DFID), is called "Rewrite

Pictured, two friends in Sudan. One is African, the other is Arabic—both are Sudanese.

the Future." Run by the organization Save the Children and backed by DFID funding, the project provides schools for children who might otherwise be unable—for a variety of reasons—to pursue an education. Such groups include girls, disabled children, and former child soldiers. The project seeks to train more teachers to a professional standard and to get parents to fully support and encourage their children's education. Teacher training has seen thousands of people, including both women and men, acquire the skills to help unschooled children catch up on years of missed lessons.

To change parental attitudes, each participating school has set up special volunteer groups. The group participants go out into local communities and spread a message about how life-changing an education can be. The project uses special methods to squeeze eight years of education into four. Following their successful use by Save the Children, the government of southern Sudan is now using these special education methods on a wider scale. Thanks to the project, total enrollment for both formal and nonformal education more than doubled from 2006 to 2007, from about 32,000 to more than 66,000. Girls' enrollment increased from nearly 12,000 to about 20,000 during this same period.

The United Nations ranks countries in a human development index (HDI). The ranking compares countries in terms of education and literacy, as well as life expectancy and standard of living. Sudan is ranked 150 among the 182 countries included in the listing. During recent years, its position has improved, but, obviously, the country still has a long way to go.

Sudan has experienced some positive recent developments. For example, it has improved relations with its neighbors, mainly Egypt and Libya, and mutual cooperation agreements have been signed with these countries. Sudan's focus on these policies, combined with more oil exploration and extraction, are the most encouraging trends for the future.

As we leave Sudan, think about its huge potential. Think about a country rich in oil, that supports universal education, wants to provide quality health care for all, and seeks to guarantee peace, security, and human rights to all of its citizens. Think about a country where children run around and play freely—without fear of landmines, rape, or violence. Think about a country that lives peacefully with its neighbors, with no refugees or displaced people. While dreaming about all these possibilities, remember and hope for the children of Darfur.

Facts at a Glance

NOTE: All data 2009 unless otherwise indicated

Physical Geography

Location	Northeastern Africa, bordering the Red Sea
Area	967,500 square miles (2,505,813 square kilometers), slightly more than one-quarter the size of the United States
Boundaries	Border countries: Central African Republic, 723 miles (1,165 km); Chad, 845 miles (1,360 km); Democratic Republic of the Congo, 390 miles (628 km); Egypt, 791 miles (1,273 km); Eritrea, 375 miles (605 km); Ethiopia, 997 miles (1,606 km); Kenya, 144 miles (232 km); Libya, 237 miles (383 km); Uganda, 270 miles (435 km)
Coastline	530 miles (853 km)
Climate	Tropical in south; arid desert in north; rainy season varies by region
Terrain	Mainly flat, featureless plain; mountains in far south, northeast and west; desert dominates the north
Elevation Extremes	Lowest point: Red Sea, 0 meters; highest point: Mount Kinyeti, 10,456 feet (3,187 m)
Land Use	Arable land: 6.78%; permanent crops: 0.17%; other: 93.05% (2005)
Irrigated Land	11,576 square miles (18,630 sq km) (2003)
Natural Hazards	Dust storms and periodic persistent droughts
Natural Resources	Petroleum; small reserves of iron ore, copper, chromium ore, zinc, tungsten, mica, silver, gold, hydropower
Environmental Issues	Inadequate supplies of potable water; wildlife populations threatened by excessive hunting; soil erosion; desertification; periodic drought

People

Population	41,087,825
Population Growth Rate	2.14%
Net Migration Rate	0.63 migrant(s)/1,000 population
Fertility Rate	4.48 children/woman
Birth Rate	33.74 births/1,000 population
Death Rate	12.94 deaths/1,000 population
Life Expectancy at Birth	Total population: 51.42 years; male: 50.49 years; female: 52.4 years
Median Age	Total: 19.1 years; male: 18.9; female: 19.2

117

Facts at a Glance

Ethnic Groups	Black, 52%; Arab, 39%; Beja, 6%; foreigners, 2%; other, 1%
Religions	Sunni Muslim, 70% (in north); Christian, 5% (mostly in south and Khartoum); indigenous beliefs, 25%
Languages	Arabic (official), English (official), Nubian, Ta Bedawie, diverse dialects of Nilotic, Nilo-Hamitic, Sudanic languages
Literacy	(Age 15 and over who can read and write) Total population: 61.1% (male: 71.8%; female: 50.5%) (2003 est.)

Economy

Currency	Sudanese pound
GDP Purchasing Power Parity (PPP)	$88.08 billion (2008 est.)
GDP Per Capita	$2,200 (2008)
Labor Force	11.92 million (2007 est.)
Unemployment	18.7% (2002 est.)
Labor Force by Occupation	Agriculture: 80%; industry: 7%; services: 13% (1998 est.)
Agricultural Products	Cotton, groundnuts (peanuts), sorghum, millet, wheat, gum arabic, sugarcane, cassava (tapioca), mangos, papaya, bananas, sweet potatoes, sesame, sheep, livestock
Industries	Oil, cotton ginning, textiles, cement, edible oils, sugar, soap distilling, shoes, petroleum refining, pharmaceuticals, armaments, automobile/light truck assembly
Exports	$12.15 billion (2008 est.)
Imports	$9.339 billion (2008 est.)
Leading Trade Partners	Exports: China, 56.3%; Japan, 30%; Indonesia, 4.9% (2008). Imports: China, 24.9%, Saudi Arabia, 8%, UAE, 5.9%, India, 5.8%, Egypt, 5.3% (2008)
Export Commodities	Oil and petroleum products, cotton, sesame, livestock, groundnuts, gum arabic, sugar
Import Commodities	Foodstuffs, manufactured goods, refinery and transport equipment, medicines and chemicals, textiles, wheat
Transportation	Roadways: 7,394 miles (11,900 km), 2,684 miles (4,320 km) is paved; railways: 3,715 miles (5,978 km); airports: 121 (19 with paved runways); waterways: 2,527 miles (4,068 km, of which 1,723 km is open year-round on White and Blue Nile rivers) (2008)

Government

Country Name	Conventional long form: Republic of the Sudan; conventional short form: Sudan; local long form: Jumhuriyat as-Sudan; local short form: As-Sudan
Capital	Khartoum
Type of Government	Government of National Unity
Head of Government	President Omar Hassan Ahmad al-Bashir (since October 16, 1993)
Independence	January 1, 1956
Administrative Divisions	25 states

Communication

TV Stations	3 (1997)
Radio Stations	14 (AM: 12; FM: 1; shortwave: 1) (1998)
Phones	356,100 main lines; 11.186 million cell phones (2008)
Internet Users	4.2 million (2008)

History at a Glance

B.C.	
<1 million years	Early humans pass through what is now Sudan.
2600 B.C.–A.D. 350	An Egyptian and Nubian civilization called Kush flourishes.
A.D.	
700s	Christianity and Islam both introduced.
1500s	People called the Funj conquer much of Sudan, and several other black African groups, including the Dinka, Shilluk, Nuer, and Azande, settle in the south.
1874	Egypt conquers Sudan.
1898–1955	Great Britain and Egypt rule Sudan as the Anglo-Egyptian Sudan.
1956	Sudan gains independence from Great Britain.
1958	General Ibrahim Abboud leads military coup against the civilian government elected earlier in the year.
1962	Civil war begins in the south, led by the Anya Nya movement.
1964	The "October Revolution" overthrows Abboud and a national government is established.
1969	Jafar Nimeiri leads the "May Revolution" military coup.
1971	Sudanese Communist Party leaders executed after short-lived coup against Nimeiri.
1972	Under the Addis Ababa peace agreement between the government and the Anya Nya, the south becomes a self-governing region.
1978	Oil is discovered in Bentiu in southern Sudan.
1983	Civil war breaks out again in the south, involving government forces and the Sudan People's Liberation Movement (SPLM), led by John Garang.
1983	President Nimeiri imposes Islamic law (Sharia).
1985	After widespread popular unrest, Nimeiri is overthrown by a group of officers; a Transitional Military Council is set up to rule the country.
1989	National Salvation Revolution takes over in a military coup.
1993	Revolution Command Council dissolved after Omar al-Bashir is appointed president.
1998	U.S. launches missile attack on a pharmaceutical plant in Khartoum, alleging that it was making materials for chemical weapons. New constitution endorsed by more than 96 percent of voters in referendum.

1999 Sudan begins to export oil.

2000 Incumbent President al-Bashir is re-elected for another five-year term.

2001 United States extends unilateral sanctions against Sudan for another year, citing its record on terrorism and human rights violations.

2002 Talks in Kenya lead to a breakthrough agreement between the government and southern rebels on ending the 19-year civil war. The Machakos Protocol provides for the south to seek self-determination after six years.

2003 In February, rebels in western region of Darfur rise up against government, claiming the region is being neglected by Khartoum.

2004 Army moves to stop rebel uprising in western region of Darfur; hundreds of thousands of refugees flee to neighboring Chad. UN official says pro-government Arab Janjaweed militias are carrying out planned killings of African villagers in Darfur.

2005 Government and southern rebels sign a peace deal, which includes a permanent ceasefire and agreements on wealth and power sharing, including oil resources. Power-sharing government is formed in Khartoum. Autonomous government is formed in the south.

2006 Sudan rejects a UN resolution calling for a UN peacekeeping force in Darfur, saying it would compromise sovereignty.

2007 Sudan agrees to allow some UN troops to reinforce African Union peacekeepers in Darfur. U.S. president George W. Bush announces fresh sanctions against Sudan. UN Security Council approves a resolution authorizing a 26,000-strong force for Darfur. Sudan says it will cooperate with the joint UN-African Union mission in Darfur.

2008 UN takes over Darfur peace force. The International Criminal Court's top prosecutor calls for the arrest of President al-Bashir for genocide, crimes against humanity, and war crimes in Darfur; the appeal is the first ever request to the ICC for the arrest of a sitting head of state. Sudan rejects the charges.

President al-Bashir announces an immediate ceasefire in Darfur, but the region's two main rebel groups reject the move, saying they will fight on until the government agrees to share power and wealth in the region.

2009   The International Criminal Court in The Hague issues an arrest warrant for President Omar al-Bashir on charges of war crimes and crimes against humanity in Darfur.

Aryeetey-Attoh, S. ed. *Geography of Sub-Saharan Africa.* 2nd ed. Upper Saddle River, N.J.: Pearson Education, 2003.

Chapin Metz, Helen, ed. *Sudan: A Country Study.* Washington: GPO for the Library of Congress, 1991.

Ferrett, Grant. "One Teacher to 100 Pupils," BBC News, August 6, 2009. Available online. URL: http://news.bbc.co.uk/2/hi/africa/8184489.stm.

Herro, Alana. "Desertification is Important Factor in Darfur Crisis." Worldwatch Institute, June 4, 2006. Available online. URL: www.world-watch.org/node/4087.

Iyob, R. and G. M. Khadiagala. *Sudan: The Elusive Quest for Peace.* Boulder, Colo.: Lynne Rienner Publishers, 2006.

Johnson, D. H. *The Root Causes of Sudan's Civil Wars.* Bloomington: Indiana University Press, 2003.

Jok, J. M. *Sudan: Race, Religion, and Violence.* Oxford, England: Oneworld Publications, 2007.

Kebbede, G. *Sudan's Predicament: Civil War, displacement and ecological degradation.* Brookfield, Vt.: Ashgate Press, 1999.

Oppong, J. R. *Africa South of the Sahara.* Philadelphia: Chelsea House Publishers, 2005.

Pettersson, D. *Inside Sudan: Political Islam, Conflict, and Catastrophe.* Boulder, Colo.: Westview Press, 1999.

Warburg, Gabriel. *Islam, Sectarianism, and Politics in Sudan since Mahdiyya.* Madison: University of Wisconsin Press, 2003.

Winter, Joseph. "No Return for Sudan's Forgotten Slaves," BBC News, Southern Sudan, Available online. URL: http://news.bbc.co.uk/go/pr/fr/-/2/hi/africa/6455365.stm.

Further Reading

Ajak, Benjamin, Benson Deng, et al. *They Poured Fire on Us from the Sky: The Story of Three Lost Boys from Sudan.* New York: Public Affairs, 2005.

Bixler, M. *The Lost Boys of Sudan: An American Story of the Refugee Experience.* Athens: University of Georgia Press, 2006.

Carney, Timothy, Victoria Butler, et al. *Sudan: The Land and the People.* Seattle, Wash.: Marquand Books, 2005.

Clammer, Paul. *Sudan: The Brandt Travel Guide.* Chalfont St. Peter, Bucks, UK: Brandt Travel Guides, 2005.

Di Piazza, F. D. *Sudan in Pictures.* Minneapolis, Minn.: 21st Century Publishing, 2006.

Flint, J. and A. de Waal. *Darfur: A New History of a Long War.* African Arguments. London: Zed Books, 2008.

Prunier, G. *Darfur: A 21st Century Genocide.* 3rd ed. Crises in World Politics. Ithaca, N.Y.: Cornell University Press: 2005.

Steidle, B. and G. S. Wallace. *The Devil Came on Horseback: Bearing Witness to the Genocide in Darfur.* Jackson, Tenn.: Public Affairs, 2007.

Web sites

BBC News Online: Sudan Country Profile

http://news.bbc.co.uk/2/hi/middle_east/country_profiles/820864.stm

CIA World Factbook—Sudan

https://www.cia.gov/library/publications/the-world-factbook/geos/su.html

CoolPlanet: Oxfam: Sudan—People and Society

http://www.oxfam.org.uk/coolplanet/kidsweb/world/sudan/sudpeop.htm

Global Issues Sudan

http://www.globalissues.org/news/2009/10/06/3065

Human Rights Watch

http://www.hrw.org/africa/sudan

U.S. Department of State, Sudan

http://www.state.gov/r/pa/ei/bgn/2861.htm

Picture Credits

page:

10:	© Infobase Publishing
15:	Getty Images
21:	© Infobase Publishing
27:	Getty Images
35:	© Christine Osborne Pictures/Alamy
43:	Getty Images
47:	© Picture Contact/Alamy
54:	© Michael Freeman/Corbis
58:	Getty Images
63:	© The Print Collector/Alamy
69:	Getty Images
72:	© Richard BakerSudan/Alamy
77:	© Nicholas Pitt/Alamy
79:	© Stephen Morrison/epa/Corbis
84:	Richard Estall Photo Agency/Alamy
91:	Getty Images
93:	Getty Images
103:	Newscom
107:	Getty Images
109:	© Jack Maguire/Alamy
113:	Getty Images
115:	© David Myers Photography/Alamy

Index

Index

About the Contributors

JOSEPH R. OPPONG is associate professor of geography at the University of North Texas in Denton, and a native of Ghana. He has nearly two decades of university teaching experience in Ghana, Canada, and the United States. His research focuses on medical geography, the geography of disease and health care. Professor Oppong has authored numerous books for the Chelsea House MODERN WORLD NATIONS and MAJOR WORLD CULTURES series. He also has served as chairperson of the Association of American Geographers Special Interest Groups on both Africa and Medical Geography.

Series editor **CHARLES F. GRITZNER** is Distinguished Professor of Geography Emeritus at South Dakota State University. He retired after 50 years of college teaching and now looks forward to what he hopes to be many more years of research and writing. Gritzner has served as both president and executive director of the National Council for Geographic Education and has received the council's highest honor, the George J. Miller Award for Distinguished Service to Geographic Education, as well as other honors from the NCGE, the Association of American Geographers, and other organizations.